Contents At a Glance

Table of Contents

About the Author

Stephen O'Brien is an Australian-born writer and entrepreneur currently residing in Sydney after too many years in Silicon Valley. He has previously written over 30 titles across multiple editions with publishers such as Prentice-Hall and Que, including several best-selling titles. He also founded Typefi, the world's leading automated publishing system, and invented a new type of espresso machine called mypressi. He has been using Minecraft since its early days and remains astounded at the unparalleled creativity it engenders. Stephen is also the author of the internationally bestselling *The Ultimate Player's Guide to Minecraft*, published by Que.

Dedication

To Mika, who has been ever patient while I worked through endless weekends. Thank you, darling son. Your dad could not love you more.

Acknowledgments

This has been an interesting project. Having had a very varied career that has also included some 30 books, I don't think there was ever one more challenging. The mod market for Minecraft involves an astonishing cavalcade of creativity that is somewhat wild westish. So west it's somewhere over the Pacific, probably beyond any cardinal point.

Bringing some sense to the chaos has been a bit of a challenge.

It has also been a challenge for my ever-patient publisher. Thank you, Rick Kughen, for your endless patience. You can cajole the best out of anyone. Also to Tim Warner who has become my partner in crime. Seth Kerney, you didn't freak out even as things went down to the wire. Not sure if I'd ever be able to exude such control.

But, finally, I want to thank a team that it has been my privilege to know for many years: Alex and Hayley Smith. They took on multiple chapters, made numerous contributions, and are truly delightful in every way. Thank you so much to you both. This book wouldn't exist without you.

One last person, but not the least by any stretch. Preeti Davidson. You have given me everything one could want. You are God's gift. (That last is for your mother.)

Thank you everyone. Reader, I truly hope you enjoy this work and find much delight herein.

We Want to Hear from You!

As the reader of this book, *you* are our most important critic and commentator. We value your opinion and want to know what we're doing right, what we could do better, what areas you'd like to see us publish in, and any other words of wisdom you're willing to pass our way.

We welcome your comments. You can email or write to let us know what you did or didn't like about this book—as well as what we can do to make our books better.

Please note that we cannot help you with technical problems related to the topic of this book.

When you write, please be sure to include this book's title and author as well as your name and email address. We will carefully review your comments and share them with the author and editors who worked on the book.

Email: feedback@quepublishing.com

Mail: Que Publishing
            ATTN: Reader Feedback
            800 East 96th Street
            Indianapolis, IN 46240 USA

Reader Services

Visit our website and register this book at quepublishing.com/register for convenient access to any updates, downloads, or errata that might be available for this book.

Introduction

Minecraft has become one of the most talked about gaming titles in recent years. It has, quite remarkably, reached across all walks of life. In a surprisingly short time, it has gained footholds in educational institutions (K–12 and beyond), in rehabilitation centers, and in many other markets where a traditional game would never dare tread.

But what do you do after you've gained your own foothold in the *Minecraft* world? You've survived, plundered, and mined your way through the hills, dungeons, and temples; fought a tough but successful battle with the Ender Dragon; and taken home the prized Dragon Egg. What next?

Well, that's where the fun really begins... and is precisely the source of so much of *Minecraft*'s enduring appeal.

Many of the features included in the standard *Minecraft* installation—redstone wiring, the ability to create complex automated mob farms, and the ability to use standard features in very creative, unexpected ways—makes *Minecraft* the ultimate sandbox game. Add to that downloadable custom-crafted adventure maps, the massive multiplayer servers whose customizations add trading systems, mini-games, and arguably entire societies, and the game becomes a whole other world.

But even that isn't the end of the story. Incredible add-ons provide *Minecraft* with goals and creative capabilities that are far more numerous than those built in to the standard game. These include taking *Minecraft* into the industrial age, all the way to nuclear power, high-speed rail, signaling systems, pipes that automate crafting and shift supplies across the landscape, and so much more. These alone, which are free to download, give the game an enduring playability that goes far beyond the original premise.

However, as with everything *Minecraft*, the discovery of these things is by no means easy. Their documentation is scattered across the Internet in a mish-mash of YouTube videos and enthusiastic wiki sites that, as a result, lack cogency. Although this is certainly no fault of the sites, among this turgid churning of possibility, there has been no single guide or site that can lead *Minecraft* players with surety—and a set of clear tutorials—through the extraordinary, awe-inspiring age of wonder that is *Minecraft* beyond the basics.

Thus, this book, is written to delight you in a process of discovery, quickly help you on your way, and leave you amazed at how much further you can go in a game that you may well have thought you'd already completed.

Become a *Minecraft* Expert!

Go far beyond *Minecraft*'s initial game with this ultimate guide by your side. You'll learn to use the standard features in amazing, new ways, and a whole lot more:

- Easily install mods and manage *Minecraft* versions, games, and profiles.
- Automate all aspects of your mining, harvesting, and building tasks.
- Generate infinite ores on demand.
- Build mob spawners and traps for fast experience gains and a wealth of item drops.
- Create gorgeous 2D and 3D art.
- Add beautiful aesthetics to any building or construction.
- Run redstone as it should be run, with timed circuits, combination locks, and other exciting creations.
- Take *Minecraft* into the industrial and nuclear ages, and gain numerous new goals, tools, and capabilities.
- Run connected trains and bore tunnels.
- Share your creation with the world and learn how the professionals capture their videos and overlay audio.

What's in This Book

Go far beyond the basics with a whole new set of tips, tricks, and strategies. Each chapter in this book focuses on a key aspect of the game, from initial survival to building an empire. Make the most of your *Minecraft* world today:

- Chapter 1, "Getting Started," goes beyond the *Minecraft* launcher to help you install mod packs and access all kinds of advanced functionality.
- Chapter 2, "Automated Produce Farms," contains the best techniques I've found (in too many gameplay hours) to create self-sustaining systems that deliver constant results, hands off. You can then sort and stock chests with the results using rails, minecarts, and some very neat tricks.
- Chapter 3, "Mining and Ore Generators," removes the need for mining. Build an endless supply of cobblestone, and create portals to The Nether without searching for diamonds.

- Chapter 4, "Mob Farms, Traps, and Defense," creates an endless supply of items and experience points. Mob grinders remove the grind and give you endless drops.

- Chapter 5, "Advanced Construction," moves into awesome building tips that focus on aesthetics. Create 2D and 3D art, decorate with style, and create trees and natural-looking terrain. Use terraforming tools to make huge changes to your world.

- Chapter 6, "More Power to You," takes *Minecraft*'s redstone and delivers a jolt of creativity. Build a combination lock to protect your fortress, learn rail switch designs, and take power to a new level.

- Chapter 7, "Empire Building with BuildCraft," takes on one of the most complex mods. You'll learn how to sort with simplicity, dig huge quarries, shift oil with pumps, refine fuel, and power massive engines.

- Chapter 8, "Titans of IndustrialCraft," will help you create new plant species, build powerful new weapons and tools, and even create a nuclear power station.

- Chapter 9, "Rolling with Railcraft," brings a bevy of enhancements to the minecart system. Let's just say that it will keep you on track.

- Chapter 10, "Recording and Sharing," will help you publish to the world. Three of the Top 10 YouTube channels are run by regular Minecrafters. You'll learn about the right hardware and software, how to plot camera paths, overlay audio, and publish like a professional.

- Chapter 11, "Building Your Own Adventure," is your game within the game. Learn to create a map you can share with others and then fill it with hidden extras (including teleportation). It's the perfect, fun way to terrify noobs.

There's a lot herein—a cornucopia of tips, tricks, and very cool stuff that extends *Minecraft* in surprising and very fun ways.

How to Use This Book

Throughout this book, you'll see that I have called out some items as Notes, Tips, and Cautions—all of which are explained here.

NOTE

Notes point out ancillary bits of information that are helpful but not crucial. They often make for an interesting meander.

TIP

Tips point out a useful bit of information to help you solve a problem. They're useful in a tight spot.

CAUTION

Cautions alert you to potential disasters and pitfalls. Don't ignore these!

Getting Started

In This Chapter

- Set up customized profiles.
- Launch earlier versions for backward compatibility.
- Separate *Minecraft* installations to protect worlds.
- Start with a full set of bundled mods.
- Back up saved worlds.

Minecraft is less of a game and more of a system containing numerous moving parts moving in close concert. If you just play the standard game, this probably won't cause you any concern, but if, as I show you in this book, you start to extend *Minecraft* in a variety of interesting ways, you'll need to know how to access different versions of the game, save your game worlds for later restoration, and perhaps even launch *Minecraft* in a completely new way.

It's not absolutely necessary you read this chapter to move on to the rest of this book, but you'll find some great steps and tips here for keeping everything working just the way it should as you break new ground, and it will definitely make it easier to install the various modifications required in later chapters.

This chapter assumes that you have purchased and installed *Minecraft* and have entered your login credentials so that you can get started.

Managing *Minecraft*

Unlike many other games that are released in an essentially final form, pending the occasional patch, *Minecraft* is a work in progress: a movable feast. The Swedish developers Mojang (pronounced *moyang*) have rapidly evolved the software's features and architecture. At the same time, fans of the product have also been busy producing thousands of mods (that is, *modifications*, add-on code that extends *Minecraft* in ways Mojang may not have intended), developing complicated multiplayer servers with their own special mods that require counterparts on the client side, and creating downloadable interactive adventure maps with yet again their own requirements.

NOTE

What's a Mod to Do?

Put simply (which is somewhat disingenuous because there is actually nothing too simple about mods), a mod can add an enormous range of features, functionality, and gameplay elements. Some mods change the landscape; others add different animals or change character animations. Some add a mapping system whereas others change the way the inventory works, or dot the landscape with hosts of new buildings and ruins. The most extensive add entire new items, systems, and interactions to the game—from powerful replacements for redstone to the implementation of industrial and nuclear ages. I go into the specifics of quite a few in the latter half of this book.

This leads to a complex interaction between all those moving parts. First, *Minecraft* itself undergoes automatic upgrades, and the mods always lag behind the update cycle, sometimes by years, leading to incompatibilities. Adventure maps are also built for specific versions of *Minecraft*. It is, quite frankly, impossible to keep them all behaving nicely without a lot of tearing of hair from their attendant follicles. In addition, playing on a highly customized competitive server with the wrong mods installed can get a hapless player banned—it's a way to prevent cheating—and, as is often the case, mods themselves also tend to conflict, tromping over each other's territory, with the potential to also corrupt precious saved games or just prevent *Minecraft* from launching.

That being said, not everyone uses multiple mods, so before getting into that, let me take you through some neat tricks you can perform with the standard Minecraft Launcher to ensure you can at least have the right version started for a particular multiplayer server or maybe just one mod in particular.

Launch Control

The Minecraft Launcher serves a number of different functions, some of them crucial. Its primary purpose is to store the login information associated with your *Minecraft* account, download and update the program files (including itself), and launch the game. But beyond that it also allows you to create individual profiles so that you can launch specific versions of the game with a few customized parameters. You can also use the launcher to access *snapshots*—pre-releases of the next version of the game—typically pried from the hands of the developers at Mojang on a weekly basis.

When you start the Minecraft Launcher, you'll see a screen similar to that shown in Figure 1.1, although of course with your own login name. I'm sure you're already very familiar with that process.

We're going to take your current profile and do some interesting things.

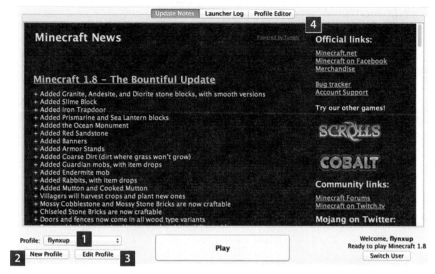

FIGURE 1.1   The standard Minecraft Launcher enables the creation of multiple profiles that in turn can become different game instances.

1. Select a predefined profile.
2. Create a new profile (copying the parameters of the one currently selected).
3. Edit the selected profile.
4. View, edit, and delete all profiles.

First, just to get warmed up, let's create a profile that will always download the latest experimental builds. These are the snapshots released by Mojang on an almost weekly basis, give or take. They always contain bugs and can corrupt saved games, so it's definitely safest to keep their worlds apart. Follow these steps and refer to Figure 1.2:

1. Click **New Profile**. You'll see the screen shown in Figure 1.2, although with your own login name as the "Copy of...."

2. Change the **Profile Name** to **Snapshots**.

3. Select **Game Directory** and , if you are using OS X, add **"/saves/snapshots"** to the end of the file path already displayed for you. If you are using Windows, add "\saves\ snapshots" instead. Also, don't edit the entire path to match that shown in Figure 1.2. Adding the suffix creates a directory called "snapshots" under the standard directory within *Minecraft*'s application folder that is already used for saving worlds and resource packs. Just adding "/snapshots" on its own would create the directory within the main *Minecraft* application folder, and potentially interfere with those already in use by *Minecraft*. Remember to add "/saves/", or "\saves\" on Windows, to the path of any other custom directories you add for other profiles.

4. Select **Enable experimental development versions ("snapshots")** and click **Yes** in the warning dialog that pops up.

5. Ensure the drop-down for **Use version** is set to **Use Latest Version**. If you click the drop-down, you'll see all the latest snapshots listed. They are named using the year and week of the year, and then alphabetically for any releases within that week. For example, 14w25b means 2014, week 25, and the *b* signifies the second release in the week. Incidentally, with **Enable experimental** disabled, this drop-down simply shows the version numbers of each final release.

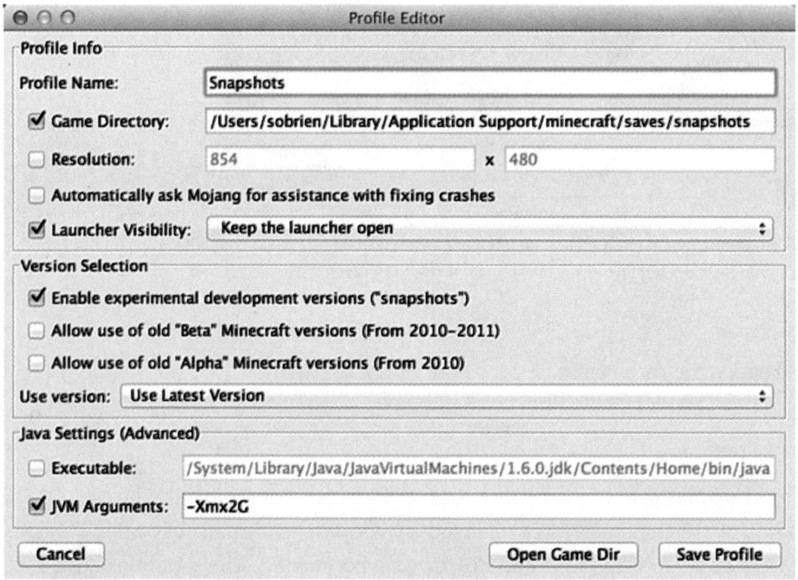

Profile Editor

Profile Info

Profile Name: Snapshots

☑ Game Directory: /Users/sobrien/Library/Application Support/minecraft/saves/snapshots

☐ Resolution: 854 x 480

☐ Automatically ask Mojang for assistance with fixing crashes

☑ Launcher Visibility: Keep the launcher open

Version Selection

☑ Enable experimental development versions ("snapshots")

☐ Allow use of old "Beta" Minecraft versions (From 2010–2011)

☐ Allow use of old "Alpha" Minecraft versions (From 2010)

Use version: Use Latest Version

Java Settings (Advanced)

☐ Executable: /System/Library/Java/JavaVirtualMachines/1.6.0.jdk/Contents/Home/bin/java

☑ JVM Arguments: -Xmx2G

Cancel   Open Game Dir   Save Profile

FIGURE 1.2 Creating a custom profile.

There are quite a few other optional settings:

- **Resolution**—Sets the width and height of the gameplay window. Note that you can also do this in the game by using the standard window-sizing controls, and this setting has no effect on the resolution when you're playing with full-screen mode turned on in game through **Options... Video settings**. (I prefer this mode for its more immersive experience.)

- **Automatically ask Mojang for assistance with fixing crashes**—Selecting this will send bug reports to Mojang, although don't expect them to contact you with any direct assistance. It will, however, help them stabilize the game.

- **Launcher Visibility**—I always set this to **Keep the launcher open**, making it easier to quit the game and restart with a different profile. If you're playing on a laptop, you'll notice

Minecraft is quite a battery drain, so being able to easily quit when off main power, but then restart when back on, is quite handy.

- **Allow use of old "Beta" and "Alpha" versions**—You can take *Minecraft* all the way back to the very first public release. It can be interesting to look at from an historical or even nostalgic perspective, but otherwise you may as well leave these unselected.

- **Java Settings (Advanced)**—It's possible to run *Minecraft* under a different Java virtual machine, but I don't recommend messing with this. However, JVM Arguments is more useful because it sets the maximum amount of RAM available to the game. The default **-Xmx1G** sets aside a total of 1GB of RAM (as indicated by the "1G" at the end). If you play with mods or high-resolution resource packs, you will probably want to increase this, although don't go higher than about half your system's total RAM. If you have 8GB, changing this to **-Xmx4G** will provide a total of 4GB to the game. Generally speaking, there's no reason to go above 2GB, or **-Xmx2G**.

When you've finished adjusting the settings, click **Save Profile** to return to the main Launcher window, ensure the Snapshots profile is selected in the Profile drop-down, and click **Play**.

If you've never played this snapshot before, the launcher will download the required files and start *Minecraft*.

Create any kind of new world, call it something recognizable (such as "Latest Snapshot"), let it load, and then quit back out to the launcher.

Let's find that saved world. This part is easy.

Click **Edit Profile** once more and then click **Open Game Dir**. Your file manager will open with the snapshot directory selected. There, you'll find a directory called saves, where you'll see your new world.

NOTE

Getting Resourceful

Resource packs are stored in the same folder as the saves directory. To make resource packs available under this profile, and to enable the option in game to open the resource pack folder, you will need to either copy an existing folder into the directory, at the same level as the saves directory, or create a blank one. In either case, just ensure it is named "resourcepacks" so the in-game button will open it correctly. Make a resource pack available by then copying it into that folder.

You can copy that world's folder to any kind of a backup system to create point-in-time "snapshots" of your world, just in case you need to restore your world at some point. You can also copy it between different PCs. Actually, you can also copy it into the directory of a multiplayer *Minecraft* server and rename the folder to "world" to make that the world the server delivers to anyone logging in.

There are only two other sections to the launcher. Click **Development Console** at the top to view a running log of messages from the server and client. (The *Minecraft* client—the part you use—runs on top of an underlying server, even when you aren't connecting to an actual server elsewhere.) This console isn't interactive, and is primarily useful for debugging purposes for mod developers.

The other tab, **Profile Editor**, provides a list of all current profiles. Double-click any profile to open the Profile Editor window you used earlier. Right-click a profile for a quick access menu from which you can add, edit, and delete profiles, and also open the selected profile's game folder.

Mod Management

As you've just seen, it's possible to create unique configurations with the standard launcher, each with their own set of saved worlds and resource packs, but this doesn't solve problems involving mod management (which can be like herding cats) because each profile, even if set to a unique directory, still launches the same instance of *Minecraft*. It is possible to overcome this manually. You'll find instructions at http://minecraft.gamepedia.com/Mods/ Installing_mods. However, that's a lot of work. Fortunately, the community set out to solve this, and they've come to the rescue in two ways:

■ **Custom launchers**—Custom *Minecraft* launchers make it easy to manage multiple installations (usually called *instances*) of the software, resource packs, and so on, as well as their installed mods. This allows you to choose the specific mods you want to use in each instance, creating your own custom version of the game without fear of it conflicting with a standard, or "vanilla," *Minecraft* installation or any other for that matter.

NOTE

Plain Vanilla, or Something Fancy?

Vanilla, in a technology context, refers to software that is not customized in any way. In other words, it runs just as originally intended. Mods and resource packs adjust *Minecraft* and can completely change the gameplay—so one of these versions of *Minecraft* is no longer plain vanilla but something fancier...maybe they should be called Ice Cream Sundaes?

- **Modpack installers**—Modpacks combine a carefully curated collection of mods with the right *Minecraft* version to ensure the compatibility of the entire set, leading to versions of the game that look toward specific gameplay targets. For example, one modpack might be designed to play on a certain server whereas another may be put together for an adventure map. Still others could simply set out to form a crafted playing experience targeting technical or magical elements, or different types of survival genres.

Let's look at them both.

Custom Launchers

Customer launchers help smooth out the experience of installing mods into particular instances of *Minecraft*. There all sorts of reasons for having multiple instances, including the following:

- **Sandboxing**—Each *Minecraft* instance has its own worlds, resource packs, and mods, preventing any possible cross-contamination between different versions.

- **Convenience**—One-click loading of mods, and the ability to turn them on or off with a check box.

- **Flexibility**—Even the same version of *Minecraft* can have its own instance, so one may focus on a particular set of mods chosen to suit a particular style of gameplay, such as technical construction, and another may target a complete different style, such as a different survival experience with new hostile and friendly entities.

There are many custom launchers. Some of the more popular, such as Magic Launcher, replicate the standard Minecraft Launcher with additional options to enable the aforementioned points. Others take a completely different tack. The one I'd most highly recommend is MultiMC. (As a side note, the modpack launchers discussed next also permit the creation of a single vanilla *Minecraft* instance, but their interfaces are not quite so slick as MultiMC.)

The point to MultiMC, shown in Figure 1.3, is that it makes creating custom *Minecraft* instances elegantly easy. It works on Windows, OS X, and Linux, and is remarkable intuitive.

You can download MultiMC from http://multimc.org. Once it is installed and opened, you'll see a blank window waiting for new instances. (On OS X you may need to hold down the Control key, click the icon, and select **Open**. If you see a window listing Java virtual machines, just ignore it and click **Open** again.)

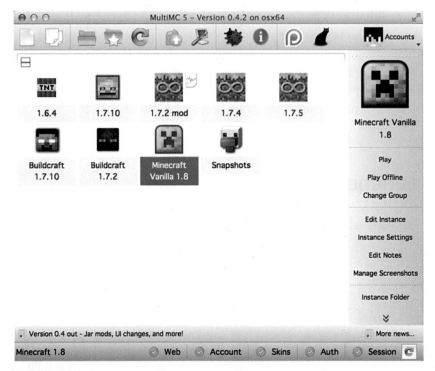

FIGURE 1.3   The MultiMC main window.

The first thing you should do is add your Mojang or *Minecraft* account:

1. Click the **Accounts** menu in the top-right corner of the main window and select **Manage Accounts** to open the window shown in Figure 1.4.

2. Click **Add**, enter your Mojang or *Minecraft* account login details, and then click **OK**. MultiMC will attempt to authenticate your account and, if successful, you'll see it added into the Manage Accounts window. Click **Close** to return to the main screen.

3. Now click the **Add a new instance** icon in the top-left corner of the toolbar.

4. In the next window, provide a name for the instance and then choose the version from the pop-up menu. You'll see both primary releases and snapshots in the list. Click **Refresh** if you want to use the latest snapshot but don't see it listed.

5. Click **OK**, and MultiMC will download the required files from Mojang.

That's all there is to it.

FIGURE 1.4   The MultiMC account management window.

The margin down the right side of the main window provides most of the primary functionality. Click the double-arrow at the bottom of the margin or increase the window size if you can't see all the entries listed next:

- **Play**—Play the instance in standard online mode, allowing access to multiplayer servers.

- **Play Offline**—Launch *Minecraft* in offline mode. Note that you can still connect to shared games via a LAN, such as your local Wi-Fi network; however, you will have had to at least once started *Minecraft* in standard online mode in order to play offline.

- **Edit Notes**—Add notes to this instance, perhaps for future reference.

- **Change Group**—Define a new group name for this instance, or assign it to a different group. You can use groups to keep vanilla versions of *Minecraft* grouped separately from those created with particular mods.

- **Manage Screenshots**—You can take screenshots within *Minecraft* by pressing F2 (or fn+F2 on OS X). These are all stored in the screenshots folder, which you'll find by opening the Instance Folder (see later in this list). MultiMC includes the convenient capability to automatically upload screenshots to Imgur.com (see Figure 1.5), making it easy to embed the screenshot in a blog or other kind of website, to share with others on the usual suspects of social networking sites, and to download in the future.

FIGURE 1.5 MultiMC can upload screenshots to Imgur for easy sharing online.

- **Edit Instance**—Opens the Edit Instance window. From here, you can switch this instance to a new version of *Minecraft*. You'll use this quite often if you access *Minecraft* snapshots. Remember, though, to click **Refresh** in the version-listing window to ensure the latest releases become available—MultiMC doesn't check the latest listings on its own. You can also install Forge, LiteLoader, or add other types of mods. See the upcoming section "Adding Mods to MultiMC" for more on this. Note that all the settings here are accessible from the main MultiMC window or from the Edit Instance window.

- **Instance Settings**—Adjust this instance's runtime settings, including screen size, memory reservation, and so on. You saw these when first defining this instance, but definitely revisit them if you, for example, load in some large mods and find *Minecraft* starting to struggle with the default memory settings.

- **Edit Notes**—Write and store notes if you're memory needs a jog on this particular instance.

- **Manage Screenshots**—Review and upload screenshots to Imgur.

- **Instance Folder**—Click to open this instance's main application folder; then open the Minecraft folder to access folders for screenshots, saved games, resource packs, and mods.

- **Config Folder**—This folder stores a mod's configuration files. These are typically plaintext folders with a .cfg extension. You can open the files and edit them in any plaintext editor and usually adjust the behavior of a mod. Figure 1.6 shows an example of the railcraft mod's main configuration file. These files provide a fascinating customization of a mod's settings and are well worth exploring—although you won't see anything in this folder until you install your first mod.

- **Delete**—Remove this instance, including all downloaded game files, saved worlds, mods, and screenshots. Obviously, use this with caution because deletion is permanent.

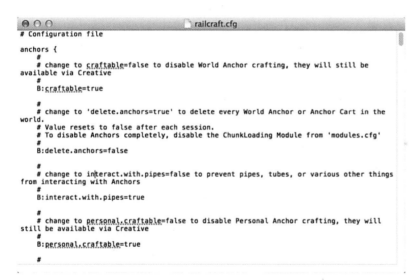

FIGURE 1.6   Railcraft's configuration file accessed from the config folder.

That covers MultiMC's main functionality, except for the most important part of all: adding mods.

Adding Mods to MultiMC

Although v1.8 of *Minecraft* promises to introduce an API that will provide compatibility between all mods, chances are you'll want to use mods with prior versions because it will take quite some time for them to be rewritten to use the new API. In fact, they'll need to be rewritten almost from the ground up, and this could take a year or two for the more complex mods. Meanwhile, Forge provides an API system that works incredibly well (see the note "Forging a Path").

Because most mods are going to change with v1.8, I'm going to list links for the 1.7 release. Create an instance for v1.7.2. Note that the mods may also work in later versions.

Open the **Edit Instance** window and click **Install Forge**. Choose the latest Forge version from the list that opens, ensuring the version number shown in the Minecraft column matches that of your instance. (Click **Refresh** if you're not seeing the one you need.) Then click **OK** to download the Forge files from the online repository.

You'll see another API system called LiteLoader. This is used for mods that don't change gameplay but add items to the *Minecraft* client, such as an in-game map and the like. It works perfectly alongside Forge and therefore can also be installed, but it's unnecessary unless you have a specific mod that requires it. For example, many of those included in the VoxelModPack use LiteLoader. Just check the dependencies when you download mods and then install LiteLoader if needed, although the VoxelModPack included in the Technic Launcher discussed in the next section will install its own instance along with LiteLoader.

Now that you have Forge loaded, you can go ahead and install mods. Click the **Loader Mods** tab. You'll see a window similar to that shown in Figure 1.7.

NOTE

Forging a Path

Minecraft v1.8 has undergone a significant redevelopment that has shifted mods from the current haphazard approach of replacing or extending core *Minecraft* code to a new system better organized under an application programming interface (API). Even so, it's going to take time for the mod authors to update their code to use this new API, and there is no guarantee that all mods will even go through the update. Some very useful ones also end up orphaned because their authors move on to other projects. Therefore, even with the brand-spanking-new API, you'll more than likely still need to create unique *Minecraft* instances to access earlier mods. Forge has solved the compatibility problems by inserting its own API into the code. Mods that use Forge then just talk to Forge rather than *Minecraft* itself, and they therefore tend to get along.

FIGURE 1.7   MultiMC's mod management window.

Time to get some mods. There are thousands, but let's install just a few key mods and a resource pack. Use the following list, with the shortened URLs shown in parentheses, to download them:

- **Optifine**—This mod vastly improves *Minecraft*'s graphics and allows the use of high-resolution texture packs. Download from http://optifine.net/downloads (http://goo.gl/ztGSVs). Scroll down the page and select the version for *Minecraft* 1.7.2.

- **VoxelMap**—This mod displays an in-game map. Go to the following link and download the Forge/FML version for 1.7.2 at http://www.minecraftmods.com/voxelmap/ (http://goo.gl/8BqWzO).

- **NotEnoughItems**—NEI adds a swathe of new controls to the standard inventory screen, accessed with the E key, making it much easier to select items in creative mode as well as to discover the crafting recipes in the survival modes. You'll need to download NEI

and also a mod support library called CodeChickenCore. Download both from http://
www.chickenbones.craftsaddle.org/Files/New_Versions/links.php (goo.gl/lBeYCl).

The mods will save to your downloads folder. If the download web page takes you to AdFly,
just wait the five required seconds and then click **Skip Ad** in the top-right corner of the
page.

Back in MultiMC, click **Add** in the Loader Mods window and select the files. Click **Close**
and double-click the 1.7.2 instance to start *Minecraft*.

If *Minecraft* crashes when you try to start a new world, go back to the instance **Settings**, click
the **Java** tab, and select **Java Settings** and then **Auto-Detect**. Ensure the Java version is at
least 1.7 and try again. If you still have issues, try downloading the latest Java version from
Java.com.

Let's add one more thing: a resource pack to change all the in-game textures. One of the
more complete is the ChromaHills resource pack. You can download it from http://www.
chromahills.com/forum/downloads.php (http://goo.gl/oHB6iX).

Open the instance settings once more, click the **Resource packs** tab and then click **Add**.
Select the ChromaHills ZIP file to copy it to the folder.

Restart *Minecraft* from within MultiMC, click **Options**, and then click **Resource Packs…**.

If you don't see the ChromaHills pack listed, as shown in Figure 1.8, then open the
resources folder and ensure it is unzipped; then head out and back into the resource packs
settings and it should appear. Make it active and click **Done**.

FIGURE 1.8 Click the arrow shown on the resource pack icon to copy it to the
right side and make it active.

Now that Optifine is installed, you'll also find numerous additional options in the video settings. Take a look through the groups called Details, Animations, Quality, Performance, and Other and set those you'd like to **Fancy**, or turn others **On**. Figure 1.9 shows the new texture pack.

FIGURE 1.9   Minecraft with the ChromaHills resource pack installed.

TIP

More Mods

So many mods are available for *Minecraft* that it can be difficult choosing those that will add the most to the experience. I focus on a few in later chapters that really do transform the game in fascinating ways, but there are also others that provide something of a helping hand, or just add minor modifications that are also fun, functional, or simply fabulous. You can download mods from many places, but one of the best is http://www.planetminecraft.com/resources/mods/. It provides a way to filter the list by a specific *Minecraft* version, and also to view the most popular downloads. Try to keep to those that support Forge to ensure there are no conflicts.

Modpack Installers

Although MultiMC provides a way to install custom versions of *Minecraft* already loaded to the hilt with various mods, there's no need to install them all independently. Modpack installers download all the required mods along with a version of *Minecraft*, creating a launcher where everything has already been verified to work happily together.

You can install as many of these as you like without any risk of incompatibilities. Try any of the following:

■ **Technic Launcher**—This mod pack, shown in Figure 1.10, is a catchall for many others. It started as a single pack called Tekkit, but now includes numerous others—at this writing a total of 109 mods all working together perfectly. Just to give you a taste of the sheer level of the expansion, Tekkit itself includes Galacticraft (fly to the moon and mars, build a space station, and so on), Railcraft (see Chapter 9, "Rolling with Railcraft"), Buildcraft (see Chapter 7, "Empire Building with BuildCraft"), alchemy, and much, much more. The other mod packs included in the launcher tend to target different thematic elements, changing the gameplay in some very fun and interesting ways. Visit http://www.technicpack.net to download the launcher; then select a modpack from the list on the left and click **Play**. If you wish to start with Tekkit, learn more about using its different mods at http://tekkitwiki.com/wiki/Tekkit_Wiki.

FIGURE 1.10   The Technic Launcher provides a simple starting point for a huge range of different *Minecraft* experiences.

■ **Feed the Beast**—This is a nicely crafted launcher (see Figure 1.11) that includes a large range of mod packs along with downloadable maps and texture packs. Grab it from http://feed-the-beast.com/launcher. Try the Voxel pack if you want to play something very close to vanilla *Minecraft* with a few handy tools, such as the built-in map that supports your own defined waypoints (never lose track of a great find ever again) and the ability to teleport between them.

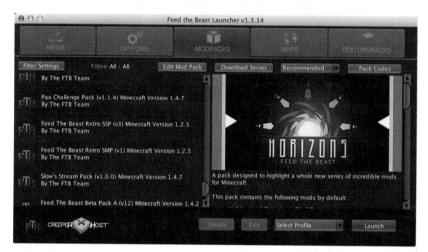

FIGURE 1.11   Feed the Beast is unusual in its inclusions of maps along with matching modpacks.

■ **ATLauncher**—ATL has become my favorite modpack installer. It provides a clean inter-face, contains numerous modpacks with detailed descriptions (see Figure 1.12), sup-ports multiple accounts, and has easy installation of Forge and Optifine. Best of all, client and fully modded servers can both be set up with the click of a button. If you don't install the others, give this one a try. It couldn't be easier. Just remember to click the **Account** tab on the right and store your *Minecraft* credentials first. Download from http://www.atlauncher.com/downloads/. If you're playing on OS X, you will need to go into your **Security & Privacy** settings in the system preferences pane and ensure that the setting **Allow apps downloaded from** is set to **Anywhere**. You'll know you need to do this if you try to open ATL and receive a message that it is corrupted. You only need to change this setting the first time you launch ATL, and you can switch it back to your preferred selection later.

FIGURE 1.12   ATLauncher is quite possibly the best modpack launcher currently available.

The Bottom Line

The marvelous forward thinking of Mojang to allow *Minecraft* to be run from multiple instances, provide access to previous versions, and support the modding community has created a gameplay experience that far exceeds the original design of the game.

Although it's possible to create you own carefully modded version, the addition of modpack launchers makes accessing new types of gameplay an absolute simplicity—and this works for running your own server or for accessing other multiplayer servers online.

Remember, though, to change the memory settings to at least 2GB if you plan to play with numerous mods or high-resolution textures bundled into resource packs. This will keep the gameplay smooth and ensure the best possible experience. The *Minecraft* you bought out of the box, the vanilla version, can become a Neapolitan of new features, functions, items, and challenges.

Some of the mods also add automated mining and farming systems, but there is still an enormous amount you can achieve in a standard *vanilla* installation. Chapter 2, "Automated Produce Farms," focuses on using redstone and minecarts to automate farms.

Automated Produce Farms

In This Chapter

- Create automated farms.
- Detect when sugar cane is ready to harvest.
- Shake loose those pumpkins and melons with the touch of a button.
- Co-opt villagers into maintaining your own farm.
- Use minecarts to automatically collect, unload, and sort gathered produce.

Farming in *Minecraft* is a necessity, at least when starting out. It's the easiest way to gather the resources needed to keep your hunger bar topped up as you battle the various mobs and make your way toward that famous showdown with the Ender Dragon. But once you've defeated the fanged one, why keep on farming? Food, at least a nibble or two, is still required because just jumping up a block will slightly deplete your health, as does sprinting, and hostile mobs are an ever-present threat no matter what you're doing.

Of course, I'm sure you already know how to set up a farm, probably arranged in an ergonomic way that makes it very convenient to reap the rewards. If not, Chapter 6, "Crop Farming," in *The Ultimate Player's Guide to Minecraft, Second Edition* will get you started.

While the basics are easy enough, this book is about achieving more sophisticated goals in *Minecraft*, and one of those is the creation of a fully automated farm. Why get your virtual hands dirty when a few pistons, a stream, and some redstone can do it all for you?

As a side benefit, this is also a useful way to learn more about the underlying logic of redstone itself. A case in point is the Block Update Detector, but more on that later.

At this writing, it's still not possible to fully automate the sowing and growing of all crops. There has never been a way to plant seeds automatically, and even though villagers finally get their hands dirty planting and gathering wheat, potatoes, and carrots, it's something of a battle to harvest the final produce before they take it for themselves. (It is not, however, one upon which I have given up!)

Before we get started, there's one very important concept to get out of the way: the BUD switch—a vital element in detecting when certain crops are ready for harvest so they can be gathered automatically.

Make Mine a BUD

The BUD (Block Update Detector) is a type of constructed switch, heavily contrived, that triggers a redstone signal when a nearby block is updated. This functionality wasn't deliberately built in to *Minecraft*, but consider it a useful side effect of the event-driven programming model behind the code itself. Whenever an event occurs in *Minecraft* that changes the nature of a particular block's space—be it placing a block in a previously unoccupied space, cactus growing into the space above, or even, surprisingly, a furnace finishing cooking or smelting an item—the code also checks the surrounding blocks to see if they need updating as well. Checking every block all of the time would simply take too much processing bandwidth, slowing the game to a crawl, so this event-driven model ensures the program continues to skip along at a reasonable rate by just taking a look at those blocks that are nearby other updates.

BUD switches exist in an inherently unstable state, somewhat like Schrodinger's cat. That is, they should be updated but aren't until a change occurs near their trigger—then the code turns its attention to them as well (observing them, if I continue the unfortunate feline's parable) and tries to resolve the instability, kicking them into action. This fires off a redstone pulse, and the code, like the peripatetic Eye of Sauron, moves on, allowing the switch to settle back into its unstable state until the next time.

BUD switches are very well documented on the Minecraft Wiki (http://goo.gl/p50VxV) and elsewhere. My goal, here, is to explain in more detail how they fit into an automated system.

Probably the easiest way to understand how this works is to build one up from basic precepts.

NOTE

Flatlanders

You'll notice a rather stark landscape in the screen captures in this and some other chapters. I've done so to help show the layout of these automated farms without any distractions confusing the picture. You can make your own quite easily because it's a good place to experiment. Just start a new world, select **More World Options...** and change the **World Type** to **Superflat**. Then click **Customize** and **Presets**, scroll down to the bottom of the list, and choose **Redstone Ready**.

Figure 2.1 shows a horizontally placed sticky piston atop a regular block with a redstone block attached to the front of the piston. Nothing too surprising here. Now place a single spot of redstone dust under the piston. Bingo! You have an instant oscillator. That piston will keep on pumping ad infinitum.

With the piston in a closed position, the redstone block powers up the redstone dust, which provides power to the block on which the piston rests, and thence to the piston itself, causing it to extend. As it extends, the redstone block moves out of range of the redstone dust, removing power from the piston, causing it to retract. Once retracted, the redstone block repowers the dust, causing the piston to extend yet again, and so on. This is all as it should be, and although it's pumping back and forth like some obsessed boxer repeatedly working on his right jab, this is, actually, a stable circuit.

FIGURE 2.1 A simple oscillating piston—the basis of the BUD.

Time for some paralysis.

Refer to Figure 2.2 and place a further regular block one step away from the redstone when it's at rest. Attach a redstone torch to the far side of that and, with your crosshairs firmly focused on the top of the torch, place a regular piston facing back toward the redstone block. You'll see the piston's jabbering instantly come to a halt. This is not because it shouldn't keep on moving; it should, but due to some vagary in *Minecraft*'s code, it doesn't. The circuit is now in an *unstable* state. The piston is waiting to move, and it will once an update strikes, but not beforehand.

Now for the main event: Go behind the sticky piston and place any kind of block on the ground; then, watching the piston, place another block on top of that. Pow! You'll see the sticky piston extend and retract. At the same time the redstone torch briefly fires up as the redstone dust behind its block becomes unpowered. (If you don't know this already, redstone torches act as inverters, remaining constantly powered unless they receive power from another source. In this case, the power from the dust that runs through the block to which they are attached is switched off as the redstone block moves out of range, allowing the torch to fire off a quick pulse before the redstone block moves back to its original position.)

FIGURE 2.2 The BUD switch primed and ready to fire.

Remove the block you just placed behind the sticky piston and another update event will fire off, activating the BUD switch once more.

Simple, eh? Well, maybe not, but it works, and let's hope the clever engineers at Mojang don't get around to fixing this any time soon because the BUD switch is useful in an incredibly wide variety of situations. Here's a brief, noncomprehensive list of some of the more interesting events that cause a block update:

- As you've seen, the placement and removal of blocks.
- Opening or closing a chest, making it possible to create a trapped chest without the change in appearance that can give away actual *trapped chests*.
- A furnace starting or finishing its smelting cycle, opening the possibility to connect the furnace to a note block that chimes when dinner's ready.
- Rails changing their orientation at a T-junction.
- The flowing past of water or lava.

- The harvesting of wheat, potatoes, and carrots.

- The growth of some plants such as pumpkins, melons, and cacti. That is the key to much of this chapter, although it is unfortunate that the growth of wheat no longer sets off a block update.

So, I hope you now have a fairly good idea as to how and why BUDs do their thing. They are surprisingly useful. Let's get into some practical examples.

Automated Cane Farms

I was tempted to title this section "Cane and Able," because cane is one of the easiest crops to farm automatically and is also quite a useful ingredient. Besides the sugar being used in several recipes, cane also acts as papyrus for the crafting of books, maps, and fireworks. Given the number of books required for a fully powered enchantment table, an automated farm definitely has its uses. Also, like melons and pumpkins, cane doesn't require replanting, and unlike them it grows in a conveniently vertical manner. This makes it the ideal target for our first BUD-based harvester.

Figures 2.3 and 2.4 show the front and back of a BUD-based cane harvester. Obviously this is a lot of work to lop the top off one strand of sugar cane, but don't worry, it's just a prototypical example. We'll extend it out shortly.

So what's going on here? It's fairly straightforward. The water is required to grow the cane, and the dirt block is just one of the several alternatives in which cane can grow; grass and sand work just as well.

Behind the cane is a spacer block and then a standard piston positioned to neatly shear the cane one block above ground level, leaving the stub behind which will then regenerate.

Given sufficient time, the cane grows up past the piston into the block next to the BUD switch, and that's when this Rube Goldberg machine swings into action. *Minecraft* performs a block update on the BUD's sticky piston, which then pushes the redstone block away from the redstone dust, allowing the redstone torch to briefly light up before the block slides back into position once more.

The redstone pulse travels along the trail until it hits the piston behind the sugar cane, extending and chopping off the upper two blocks of cane.

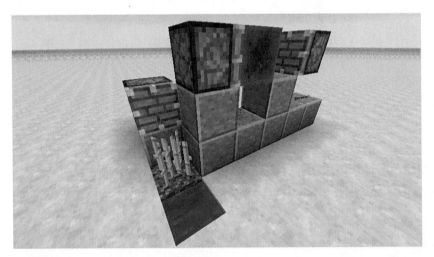

FIGURE 2.3 Automated cane farm, reductio ad absurdum.

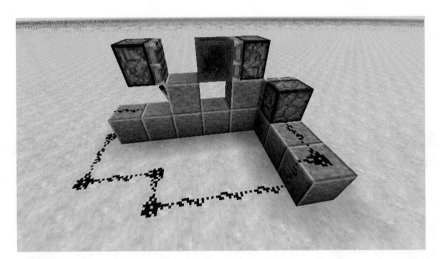

FIGURE 2.4 Behind the curtain, redstone dust delivers power from the BUD to the harvesting piston.

Let's extend the concept further. Water flows across a flat surface for a total of eight blocks, providing a commonly used extent for numerous farming layouts. Dig out the water channel until it runs for eight spaces, and lay down another seven spacer blocks behind the bed, topping each with a piston, as shown in Figure 2.5.

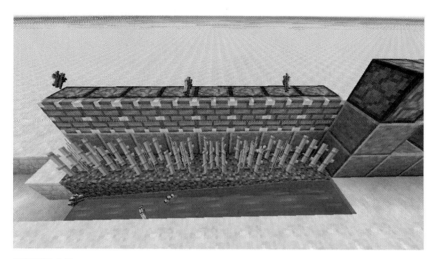

FIGURE 2.5   Extending the farm to eight blocks.

There's a little more work to do to get the pistons firing correctly. Figure 2.6 shows the layout. Run redstone along the top of blocks positioned behind each piston.

FIGURE 2.6   Powering up a plethora of pistons.

This is still not the most efficient design. It's somewhat haphazard, as you can see in Figure 2.5, with lots of sheared cane left behind, and on harvesting some of the cane will fly right across the water channel to the other side. In addition, there's no point building an automated farm that doesn't also stash the produce in a storage item such as a chest to prevent it de-spawning after five minutes. Let's build on.

TIP

Slimming Slime

There's a new type of block in town—slime. It doesn't ooze its way across the dance floor, but it does provide some compelling improvements on the standard, staid block. Slime sticks to slime, so place a single sticky piston, then one block of slime in front and another on top of that, and you'll have a stack of shearing blocks that work just like a double piston. You can do some amazing things with slime, but its one caveat in Survival is that each slime block requires nine slimeballs, and these can be a little scarce given the spawning of slime is limited to swamp biomes and only 10% of potential underground spawn grounds. Therefore, in many cases it's actually easier to just combine a piston with a single slimeball to create an additional sticky piston rather than finding all the slimeballs required to build slime blocks.

The easiest way to collect the produce is to let it flow into a hopper connected to a chest. Figure 2.7 shows the layout. Place the chest first, leaving one space between it and the stream; then move to the stream side and Shift-click the back of the chest to attach a hopper. (Just placing the hopper doesn't work: It must be connected to the chest through the Shift-click action, unless it is positioned directly above the chest.)

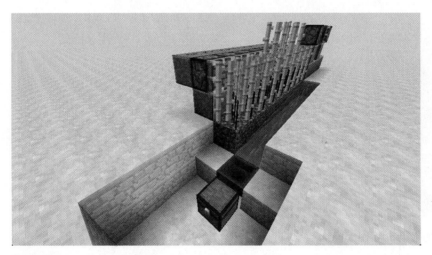

FIGURE 2.7   Use hoppers connected to a chest to pick up the produce floating down the stream.

By the way, later in this chapter I'll show you how to completely automate the collection of goods via a minecart with a hopper and transport them to a central location.

Back to our farm, there are a few other improvements to be made to prevent collected produce from falling outside the collection stream. One method is to double the width of the stream and then place a hopper at the end of that stream that is connected to the first hopper, again via a Shift-click. However, I prefer just enclosing the farm in glass, as shown in Figure 2.8.

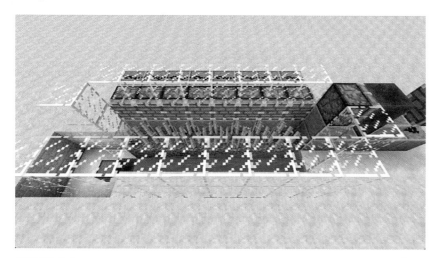

FIGURE 2.8   Don't throw stones: encasing the farm in glass.

This design still isn't quite as efficient as it could be. Typically most of the cane ends up left on the garden bed. It's actually better to build up a double-layer of pistons so an entire wall hits the cane at once. This raises the collection efficiency from three to five pieces per cycle to around 10 to 13—a huge change!

You'll see the arrangement in Figure 2.9. Note that placing a piston in the far-right position of the top row, next to the BUD switch, causes the pistons to constantly oscillate, which becomes old very fast, so leave that one out. Wiring up the two layers is easy: Just run the redstone on top of a set of blocks behind the top layer, and the lower one will trigger as well.

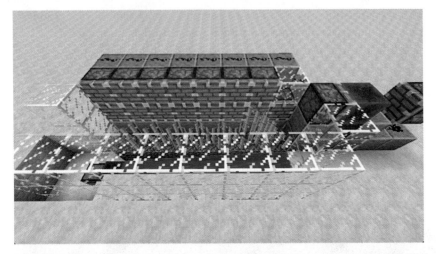

FIGURE 2.9 A double-layer of pistons provides more shearing efficiency, but make sure you leave a gap at the end, adjacent to the BUD.

NOTE

Why Not a Single-Level Farm?

If you're playing on Survival and are possibly a little hard up for resources, you might consider dropping the BUD switch down one level and just using a single-layer of pistons. Unfortunately, there's no way to make this work because you'll need a piston right next to the BUD to shear the final stand of cane that triggers the BUD. The piston's movement will then fire the BUD again, causing it to develop a constant oscillation.

Automated Collection and Transport

Using a minecart with a hopper provides a way to fully automate the collection of produce. Although a hopper doesn't store as much as a chest, having only five slots instead of 15, there are no toll roads in *Minecraft*, so it doesn't really matter how often it goes back and forth. Also, the hopper has the advantage that we can build a very simple yet fully automated collection, transport, and transfer system.

It's surprisingly easy, and oh so satisfying to see running at full steam. Let's get into the detail.

The basic principle has an elegant simplicity:

1. A comparator measures the contents of a hopper, and a comparator provides an output current when a hopper contains something.

2. A redstone torch inverts the signal and powers a rail accordingly. Powered rails are ideal for rail terminations because when unpowered they immediately slow a minecart to a stop. As long as they are at the end of a line, powering the rail will then send the cart flying in the other direction.

3. At the pickup end of the line, the inverted signal from the comparator will keep the rail unpowered if the produce hopper contains something waiting to be collected. It will then send the minecart back once all the hopper's contents have been transferred to the cart.

4. Reversing the process at the other end, a comparator is attached to the receiving hopper, which in turn is attached to a chest.

5. As soon as the minecart arrives, it immediately starts transferring items to the receiving hopper, which, as it now contains something, fires up the comparator turning off the rail.

6. The receiving hopper transfers the contents to the chest; then, the comparator stops providing a signal, which, by being inverted, powers up the rail sending the minecart back to the pickup point.

At this stage, you're probably thinking a picture or two may help.

NOTE

Getting Redstone Ready

If you don't have any familiarity with redstone and rails, consider reading Chapter 9 from *The Ultimate Player's Guide to Minecraft, Second Edition*. It provides a thorough introduction to both topics.

Figure 2.10 shows the front view of this system. Figure 2.11 shows the back, and Figure 2.12 shows it from overhead. Imagine the bottom of the U in the track extending any distance you need, with boosts provided by powered rails. The right side is the pickup end, and the left, the delivery. Produce is fed into the hopper, generally positioned at the end of a stream, which is *Minecraft*'s best equivalence of a conveyor belt. The five hopper slots can store 64 items each, or 320 items in total, so although hoppers aren't quite as capacious as chests, they're also no lightweight.

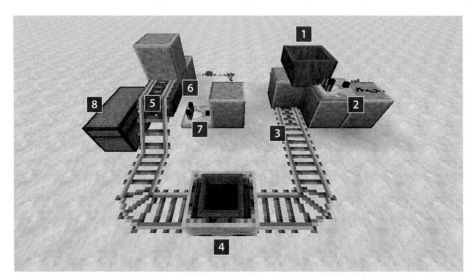

FIGURE 2.10 FedEx, meet *Minecraft*: an automated pick-up and delivery system.

1   Hopper stores items for pickup.

2   Comparator reads hopper's status.

3   Powered rail turns off when hopper contains items.

4   Minecart with hopper transfer items.

5   Receiving hopper.

6   Comparator reads signal from the receiving hopper.

7   Powered rail switches off when the hopper is receiving items.

8   Chests store goods transferred from the receiving hopper.

The view from the back (Figure 2.11) shows the two inverters: redstone torches that turn off when receiving a signal from the comparator, meaning the hoppers are not yet empty.

Finally, just for reference, Figure 2.12 provides a bird's eye view. Remember as you construct this to take care to have the comparators facing the right way. You'll also need to attach the receiving hopper to the chest by Shift-clicking the chest, and Shift-click the receiving hopper when laying the powered rail on top.

FIGURE 2.11   Some redstone torches and redstone wiring complete the picture.

1   Hopper stores items for pickup.

2   Redstone torch turns off when comparator provides a signal from the hopper.

3   The redstone torch powers this block, which powers the rail under the hopper.

4   This torch receives a signal from the comparator connected to the receiving hopper.

5   The redstone power also transfers through this block to the rail immediately behind.

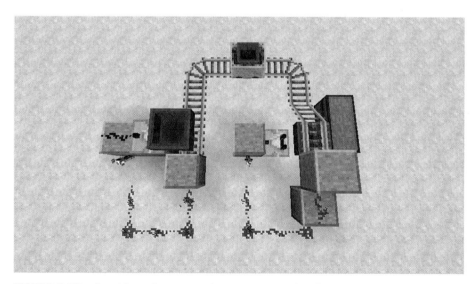

FIGURE 2.12   Looking down on the automated railway.

This is all quite easy to integrate with the cane farm, or, indeed, any farm. Figure 2.13 shows just one example for the loading station.

FIGURE 2.13　Back at the farm, this minecart is loading up with sugar cane and will soon be ready to haul it out and head back to base.

TIP

Going Postal

An automated system such as this doesn't need to just move produce between a farm and central storage. You could also use it to create a delivery system between two stations—for example, home base and another deep in a mine, sending food and tools in one direction and mined ore in the other. Because hoppers can also connect to furnaces, you could actually send just smelted items. One slight complication: The setups for receiving and delivering are quite different, so you'll need to use a detector rail connected to a T-junction at each end so that an empty minecart goes to the loading bay, and a loaded minecart goes to the delivery bay. Best of all, by replacing the hoppered minecart with an empty one, you can also go for a ride.

Automated Pumpkin and Melon Farms

Pumpkins and melons are easy to grow, but need some interesting tricks to automate. They're both quite handy as crops, with multiple uses, although once you've seen one dodgy jack-o'-lantern with a couple of levers for arms standing forlornly in a wheat field... well, you've probably seen them all. (On the other hand, jack-o'-lanterns do make an excellent underwater light source if you've run out of the makings of glowstone.)

As with much of *Minecraft*, it's the journey as much as the destination—so, yes, this will be another convoluted construction, perhaps even more so than the cane farm. Pumpkin-piston harvesters are not for the pusillanimous. You will, however, find that the system as a whole does embody useful concepts that can be used in many other places, including when creating mob traps.

As you'd be aware, pumpkin and melon seeds need to be planted on hydrated, tilled dirt. (Because the methods are the same for each, I'll just refer to pumpkins from now on, rather than pumpkins *and* melons.)

The pumpkin forms to one of the four sides of the stem. This is all a little random from the purview of automation, but some order can be brought to the chaos by blocking three of the sides with blocks, water, or other stems, leaving just one space in which the actual pumpkin can grow.

We'll start with a semi-automated farm that uses pistons to shake the pumpkin loose from its stem, and then allows water to course through, sweeping the produce into a hopper. This is a linear design, much like the cane farm.

Figure 2.14 shows the basic concept. The water hydrates the pumpkin stem and produces a pumpkin on the only block available—the dirt on top of the sticky piston. (The piston has to be sticky or the dirt block won't retract with the piston at the end of the cycle.) Moving the piston shakes the pumpkin loose.

FIGURE 2.14   A simple pumpkin-piston harvester.

Extending this out linearly for eight blocks leads to Figure 2.15. All fairly straightforward, although you'll note in the image that I've shown two ways to power the pistons. You can use repeaters to feed the power directly into each piston at the level of its base, or you can place a block beside the piston and just run redstone along the top. (You may at this point leap to the conclusion that you could also just sink a row of eight pistons into the ground and run a string of redstone beside them on top of the ground. You'd be right, and that is the simplest way to do so, as you'll see in Figure 2.16. I did, however, want to show an alternative.) I've also changed the glass blocks to polished andesite so that I can place torches on top to enable the crop to grow through the night. You can use any type of nontransparent block you prefer.

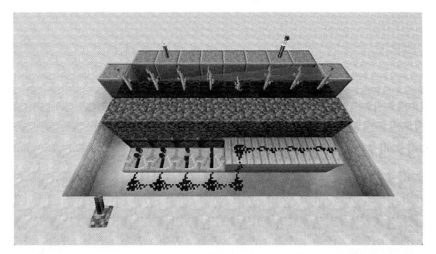

FIGURE 2.15 Extending the base design out into a string of eight.

If you wait a short while (each stem produces about three pumpkins per hour), you'll see some pumpkins appear. Pull that lever to shake them loose.

That's the harvesting done. We'll collect the produce by creating a channel above the bed. As the pistons lift, they'll push their dirt blocks up into the channel, forming the bed for the watercourse, as shown in Figure 2.16. I've used glass blocks for the sides of the channel so that maximum light can still reach the pumpkin stems—and it looks neat.

The next challenge is to create the water's source. One method is to use an elevated piston positioned at the far end of the channel that, when extended, forms the base of a water source block. Retracting the piston opens the sluice gate, allowing the water to flow down into the crop's channel, sweeping everything to the end. You can see an example of this in Figure 2.17. We're going to go for something a bit neater using a dispenser. It's a better engineering solution, and tidier all around.

Place a dispenser at the far end of the channel so that it faces toward the dirt blocks. Then right-click to open it and place a bucket of water inside.

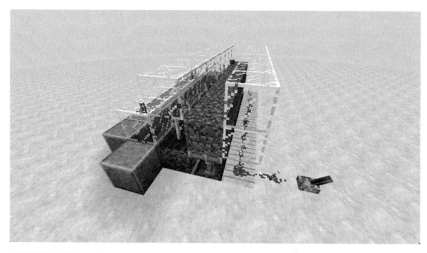

FIGURE 2.16 Creating a channel down which the harvesting water can flow. As the pistons extend, the dirt on top of each forms the base of the channel. This farm now uses a simpler design with redstone on the ground, instead of additional blocks or repeaters.

FIGURE 2.17 An elevated water source block held up with a piston. When the piston is retracted, the water can flow down into the channel.

You'll need to also place a block underneath, and then another offset as a step for the redstone wiring, and run the wiring as shown in Figure 2.18. The dispenser will be powered as long as the wire reaches the block under the dispenser.

Run the wiring back to a block with a stone button positioned close to the lever. If you need to go further than 15 blocks, place a repeater pointing in the direction of the dispenser to boost the current. Why a button and not a lever? Dispensers place the water source block directly in front upon receiving a pulse, and will retract it upon receiving a second pulse, so pressing a button to start, then stop, makes more logical sense than flicking a lever twice. Think of it as user interface design.

FIGURE 2.18 Dispensers are a more compact solution than water towers for swishing away produce.

It is, however, a little frustrating to have to push that button twice. Can we do the same with just a single push, sending two pulses with a delay between them that provides enough time to wash any produce down to the end of the stream?

Sure can—by splitting the single pulse in two. One is sent immediately and the other is siphoned off into a delay loop where it slowly wends its way along until it hits the dispenser.

There are numerous ways to build delays into redstone circuits. The simplest, and a good starting point, is to use a virtual truckload of redstone repeaters. Each repeater introduces a delay of 1/10 of a second, but repeaters also have a four-position slider that adds an additional tick each position, resulting in an up-to-four-tick delay per repeater:

1. Follow Figure 2.19 to arrange the repeaters in a caterpillar pattern.

2. With several right-clicks of the mouse, set each repeater's slider to its furthest position to add the maximum delay.

3. Add a single repeater between the two connections leading into the delay loop. It should face toward the wire leading to the dispenser. Repeaters act as a diode, only permitting current to flow in one direction. This prevents the output from the delay loop flowing back into the input of the delay loop, and thus constantly cycling for all eternity. (If you are ever in doubt about the direction a repeater is facing, you may notice a faint arrow pattern on top. The head of the arrow points in the direction the current will flow.

Alternatively, you can just remember that when the slider is in its default position, both the controls on top of the repeater are located at its head, pointing the way forward.)

4. Finish off by adding a hopper and a chest to the end of the collection area.

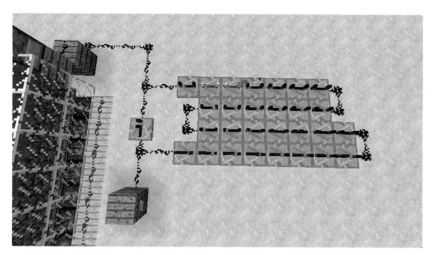

FIGURE 2.19   Turn a button into a two-pulse system using repeaters to create a delay on the second pulse. In this image you can see the current inching along the caterpillar tracks.

Using this system isn't exactly foolproof. Pushing the button with the pistons up will cause something of a disastrous flood. There is a way to fix this, ensuring the button *only* fires if the lever is powered on. It's called an AND gate. Essentially, an AND gate operates only if *both* inputs are on (see Figure 2.20). If either is off, it's a no-go. By feeding the lever into one of the inputs, and using the button for the other, you can limit the button to only operating if the lever is already on, and therefore the pistons are raised. This doesn't prevent dropping the pistons mid-cycle. In Chapter 6 , "More Power to You," I'll show you a method that solves this. Meanwhile, the AND gate is a useful safety measure, at least, so go ahead and add it to the circuit as follows:

1. Place a row of three opaque blocks.

2. Position a redstone torch on top of the first and last blocks, and a third against the back face of the middle block.

3. Place redstone on top of the middle block.

4. Connect an output from the lever to the first block and place a stone button or wooden button on the front face of the last.

5. Connect the redstone entering the repeater delay circuit back so that it meets the redstone torch attached to the middle block.

6. With the lever in the off position, pressing the button should have no effect, but with the lever switched on, both inputs contribute to allow the signal from the button to flow out the back and into the circuit heading to the dispenser and the delay loop.

FIGURE 2.20   The AND gate is a logic circuit that only provides an output when both inputs are positive.

One final addition completes this harvester: the minecart pickup system.

Connecting this harvester has just one tiny wrinkle because pistons make for a terrible termination block for railways. The train will plough halfway into them when raised, and won't zoom back on the powered rail when it has finished its pickup. Instead, feed the track in from the side, as shown in Figure 2.21. The redstone torch again inverts the signal, providing power to the rail only when there is no signal from the comparator, signifying that the hopper is empty. As soon as anything drops into the hopper, the power to the rail switches off, allowing the items to transfer.

This is by no means the full potential extent of this topic. If you look on YouTube, you'll see descriptions of fully automated slicer/dicer systems that, although not made by Ronco, offer a host of possibilities beyond basic harvesting. (Try searching youtube.com for "minecraft melon farm.") They all rely on an interesting attribute of pumpkins and melons: They conduct redstone power. By arranging the redstone so that the pumpkin or melon completes a circuit, it's possible to power up a piston to automatically harvest the crop. Figure 2.22 shows one example that makes use of the fact that pumpkins and melons can grow their goods in more than one space at a time. The two places left open are each directly in front of pistons that are waiting to pounce. The moment the pumpkin or melon appears, the circuit is completed from the redstone torch in the front middle through the hapless produce and around to the appropriate piston, which immediately either harvests the pumpkin or turns a melon into melon slices. There are hoppers under the repeaters connected to another placed under the redstone torch. (Place repeaters and torches on hoppers by Shift-clicking, just as with connecting hoppers to chests.)

This layout isn't particularly efficient: It only collects about 60% of the produce due to the rest being lost over the area occupied by the stem. However, it's fully automatic, so that doesn't really matter. Leave it long enough and it will, assuredly, deliver the goods.

FIGURE 2.21   Add a minecart station to the pumpkin farm. Bring minecarts into stations that rely on pistons by coming in from the side.

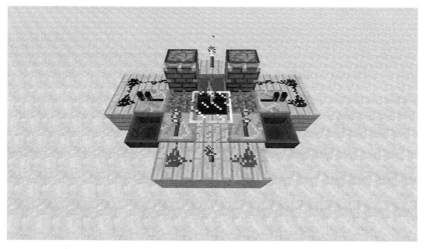

FIGURE 2.22   A fully automatic pumpkin or melon farm.

Automated Wheat, Potato, and Carrot Farms

I mentioned earlier that at this time there is no possible means for automatically sowing wheat. The question, then, is whether it is possible to use the villagers' new found ability to sow the stuff, and somehow have them do it for you but still leave you with enough time to reap the harvest before they get their hands on it. Actually, villagers don't have hands because their arms are permanently connected in a U. Perhaps they have particularly adept elbows. In any case, this has proven to be a formidable challenge.

Note that I described a semi-automated wheat farm on page 120 of *The Ultimate Player's Guide to Minecraft, Second Edition*. It uses the raised piston method to spill water across the field and sweep the crop into a collection stream at the bottom, and then across to a hopper, and thence a chest, or to await collection by a passing minecart. The same method works for potatoes and carrots, so here I'll just refer to wheat and you can substitute with your preferred root vegetable.

Switching the earlier system to dispensers would result in something like what's shown in Figure 2.23. (Note that I've deliberately left out the earlier complexity of double-pulse delay circuits, but of course you could add those the same way you would to the pumpkin harvester.)

TIP

Can You Dispense with the Dispensers?

You don't really need a row of eight dispensers to flush out a field just eight rows across. Three will do it for one field. Put one in each corner and the other in one of the two midmost positions. However, you'll have problems with longer fields where the water needs to flow down a step because any water that has to flow across a field will use up steps beyond the full seven it needs to cascade down to the next level.

For the sake of completeness, keep in mind that water flows essentially forever, so long as it drops down at least one step in every seven. Therefore, it's quite easy to extend this field to almost twice its length, or thrice, and so on, by shifting the dispensers back and up one level every seven blocks, as shown in Figure 2.24.

So, what of our salt-o'-the-earth, humble village folk, tirelessly working the fields? Let's convince them to also work for us. The only prerequisite is that you find a village, or on Creative use the villager spawn egg. I prefer the former.

Running a successful village farm is an exercise in sustainability. Villagers do not have an endless supply of seeds. They can only sow what they reap, using the additional seeds from wheat harvesting, and also replanting potatoes and carrots as they go. If you strip a village's farms to the bare earth, you'll upset the balance, forcing the village into a long, slow recovery.

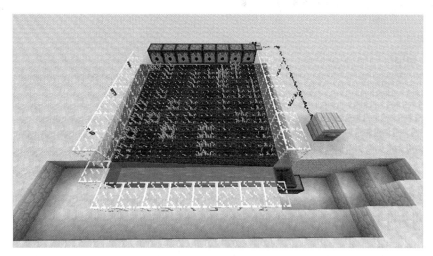

FIGURE 2.23   A full broadside of dispensers makes short work of a field of crops. You can run the redstone over a line of blocks set just behind the dispensers, similar to the pistons shown in Figure 2.6.

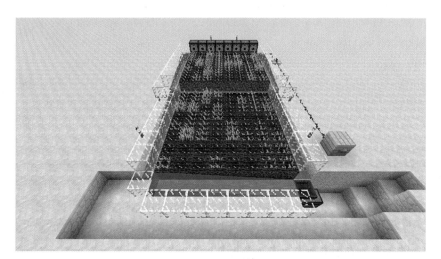

FIGURE 2.24   Extending the field back gains far more produce for the same number of dispensers, at the cost of some basic blocks and a little redstone wiring.

With these game mechanics in mind, it's best to add on to a village's farm land. Place yours adjacent to the existing farms and, once tilled, the farm villagers will plant seeds for you. Leave the other farms alone: They'll act as a constant supply of seeds so that you can regularly harvest your own field without worrying about running out of natural resources.

Figure 2.25 shows an example using dispensers to drive crops down toward a hopper and chest. Here are a few points:

- Villagers don't till soil. You'll need to do that first, and also ensure the farmland is hydrated for the fastest growth. I've hidden two water pools under the slabs running down each side.

- Why use slabs? It's important that the villagers don't jump down a full block height onto your farmland, or back on their own, because this will revert the farmland block on which they land to a standard dirt block that's untilled and therefore not suitable for planting. Using slabs for the sides protects the bed but also prevents the water from the dispensers from spilling over the side.

- Get things started by planting the first crop. After that, the villagers will take notice and look after things on their own.

- Don't expect a constant hive of activity. Be patient. Villagers take a lot of breaks, they don't work at night, and they'll even make a dash for shelter when it starts to rain.

- Protect your villagers. If you run out of farmers (the brown-smocked ones), nothing much is going to happen down on the farm. Consider placing torches throughout the surrounding area, and block off nearby caves. Zombies are a villager's natural enemy, and you should try to keep them away.

- If you time it right, you can fence or wall a villager into your farm, and any others adjacent. As long as the wall keeps out zombies and keeps the villager in, they'll become permanent farmhands and will wait out the night with only the occasional panicked dash about.

- Try as you might, it's impossible to control the crops planted unless the villagers only have access to the one type. For example, if they can only collect wheat, they'll only plant wheat. Otherwise, expect a mix of carrots, potatoes, and wheat.

- You can harvest your own farm bed as often as you like, sweeping down any grown produce along with wheat seeds and so on. Help with the replanting, and as long as you leave the other farm beds alone, you'll find a happy balance of useful produce and efficient production.

FIGURE 2.25   Adding your own farm to a village allows you to take advantage of villagers' ability to sow crops, permitting a far more automated method of farming. Note the white collar supervisor doing no work at all... typical.

Automated Sorting

Now that you have a range of automated farms and know how to collect the produce, it's time to look at one final improvement: sorting the contents of minecarts into different chests.

There's no way to imbue the minecart itself with this type of intelligence, but it can be done with hoppers and redstone, at least if the items you are sorting are stackable in an inventory slot. The idea is that by putting at least one of the items you wish to sort into each of the five slots in the hopper, no other items will be able to drop in. In other words, you're stacking the deck. In practice, it's a little more tricky because, assuming you've connected the hopper to a chest, you actually don't want it to empty completely, or that would also clear all the slots and leave the hopper open to collect items of any type. By using a comparator, it's possible to read the hopper's inventory level and then apply a current to the hopper to stop it transferring the remaining items. This requires 22 inventory units of the item you're filtering: 18 in the first slot and one each in the other four. Fortunately, the whole system is easier to set up than some of the other redstone contraptions we've been building. It works by feeding a signal strength of two from one hopper stacked with the item you wish to sort, to another, controlling the flow of items from the minecart hopper that travels above. When the first hopper drops below a signal strength of two (due to the transfer of items to the chest), the comparator lowers its output signal and, through an inverter, provides power to the lower hopper to stop any further transfer of items so the hopper's slots retain the original items used as a filtering system.

Figure 2.26 shows a complete sorting system. It works like a loom, with the minecart running across the top, similar to a shuttle—in textile terms, of course.

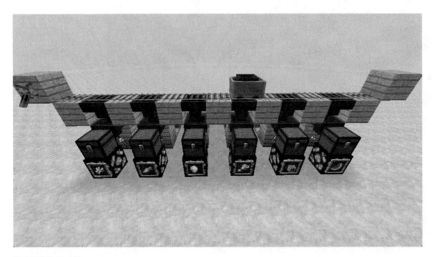

FIGURE 2.26   An item-sorting system. The minecart flies back and forth depositing its contents via item filters into each hopper, which ultimately triggers the transfer to the respective chest.

Follow these steps to build your own sorter (it's an extensible design, so you'll have no trouble at all enlarging it to handle all kinds of items):

1. Start with the base design shown in Figure 2.27. The comparator on top faces to the left, and the repeater on the bottom to the right. Place redstone on top of the two exposed blocks.

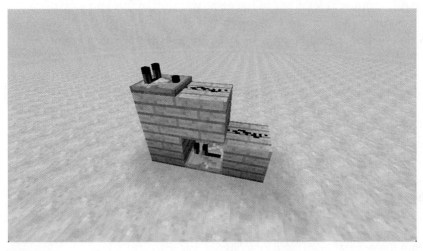

FIGURE 2.27   Each sorter begins with this sequence of base blocks. Ensure the comparator and repeater face in the correct direction.

2. Place the redstone torch as shown in Figure 2.28, followed by the redstone lamp and a chest. If you are playing on Survival and are short of glowstone, just use any other block in place of the lamp. The lamp flickers off when an item is dropped into the chest above, but this is just a dispensable dramatic touch.

3. Now for the tricky part. As you've seen, a hopper receiving a redstone signal will cease accepting and forwarding items. However, a hopper on top of another, connected to it, will drop items down regardless of that power signal. This is something of a quirk of the way the redstone system was built, because a hopper connected to another that is adjacent will respect the signal and not shuffle items through. The workaround is to ensure the upper hopper connects anywhere other than straight down to the one below. The easiest way to achieve that in this layout is to jump on top of the chest, point the crosshairs at the slender front face of the comparator, and Shift-click to place the hopper so that its outlet points to the comparator. Then, jump off and Shift-click on the back of the chest to connect another hopper to it that is directly below the first.

FIGURE 2.28 The correct connection of hoppers is the key. Ensure the topmost points away from the one underneath.

4. You're almost done. Click the top hopper to set its filter. Figure 2.29 shows the general idea. Load at least 18 of the sorting item into the first slot, and then one of each into those thereafter. This will provide the two-strength output signal that controls the lower hopper. The essential concept is that the hopper cannot accept any other item except one that can stack with those already in place, and as soon as one of those drops in, the signal increases and turns off the power to the lower hopper, allowing the item to drop through to the chest.

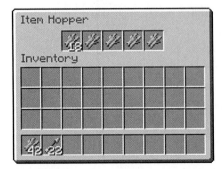

FIGURE 2.29   Sorting sorted! Just fill the slots with the item you need to filter.

5. Finally, place the rail lines and hoppered minecart across the top using a powered rail at each end to send the cart back and forth (see Figure 2.30). Place a torch underneath the rail buffer block at one end and, if you want to stop the cart now and then, a lever against the one at the other end so it can cruise to a halt against an unpowered rail. Figure 2.31 shows the other side of the sorter, for easier reference.

FIGURE 2.30   The complete sorting system. Just add sections to handle new items as required.

6. I'm going to leave the expansion of this *Minecraft* device to your own devices. Its Achilles heel is that any unsorted items will gradually build up and block the delivery cart, so you should expand it to accept all types of crops that get collected. You'll also find this system particularly helpful in Chapter 4, "Mob Farms, Traps, and Defense," where you can use it to channel the very useful drops from mobs into separate containers.

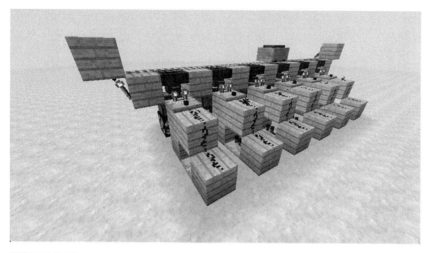

FIGURE 2.31 The business end of the sorter: You'll find it a cinch to replicate to handle all kinds of items.

Finally, a small but interesting challenge: Use the minecart unloader design to feed this one. Place a hopper above one end of the track, right over the powered rails, and then adapt the unloading station I described in "Automated Collection and Transport." Hoppers act fast, allowing minecarts to shift goods even as they are flying back and forth.

The Bottom Line

In this chapter you learned how to build an automated sugar cane farm using a BUD switch to detect when the cane is ready. You also saw how to build a fully automatic pickup and delivery system to bring your farmed goods back to base. We also got our hands dirty with semi- and fully automated pumpkin and melon farms, used pistons to shake them loose, and then created a timed flush-through to pick up the results.

Along the way, you saw a wheat field extended across a vast vista (well, not so much, but you can do so if you want) and co-opted a farming villager into planting your own field of wheat, potatoes, and carrots. Welcome to the bread basket, or the vegetable basket... or, really, whatever you care to make of it. You will, in any case, never find yourself lacking for produce again.

I hope the redstone hasn't left you feeling daunted. If you haven't used it very much in the past, it can seem quite confusing, but with practice will come not just familiarity but also an easy understanding. I must confess that when I first starting delving into the dusty red stuff, I wondered how much use it could be beyond opening doors and doing a few basic things.

I certainly wasn't intending to build a simulation of a CPU or a giant digital clock. But it's surprisingly handy once you hit situations where you need to figure out how to automate a particular process. And remember, there's a beginner's guide to redstone in Chapter 9 of *The Ultimate Player's Guide to Minecraft*, Second Edition, and I dive into it a lot more extensively in Chapter 6 in this one.

In the next chapter we'll dig into automated ore generators. Why don the hard hat and develop virtual blisters swinging that pick when you can create a range of essential ores entirely above ground?

Mining and Ore Generators

In This Chapter

- Create an endless expanse of self-healing cobblestone.
- Generate all the stone you need for massive constructions.
- Save on diamonds and create a portal on the spot without mining obsidian.

Ores are the building blocks of *Minecraft*. You can use them to create creeper-proof buildings, dwellings, and rail bridges across the sky. Actually, unless you plan to live in a mud hut, you really can't beat cold, hard stone. But why grub about in dark tunnels when you can create all the building ore you could ever possibly need, and then top it off with an overdose of some of the toughest stuff in *Minecraft*—obsidian—and do so without putting so much as a scratch on your new diamond pickaxe. It's all surprisingly easy.

Creating Cobblestone

Cobblestone is one of the most prevalent and useful blocks in *Minecraft*. As a building material it provides the same blast resistance as any other, with the exception of obsidian, which is about 200 times tougher, and the essentially indestructible bedrock. Even a wall of diamond blocks won't provide any greater protection than cobblestone against a creeper waiting outside your door.

The venerable cobbled stone is also exceptionally versatile. Cobblestone is used in the crafting of furnaces, dispensers, droppers, levers, and pistons, among other things. It can also be turned into stairs, slabs, moss stone (for that *Temple of Doom* appeal), and the usual tools.

Although cobblestone is found just about everywhere underground, it's also one of the easiest ores to automatically produce. I'll show you how to create an endless supply, and also how to turn it into an endlessly healing platform. Doing so requires a few pistons and a simple redstone clock circuit.

Cobblestone is formed when flowing water meets flowing lava at the same level, as shown in Figure 3.1. (Flowing water meeting a lava source block produces obsidian, and flowing water dropping on top of flowing lava creates stone.)

Creating a supply of cobblestone therefore requires just a bucket each of lava and water.

FIGURE 3.1 Cobblestone forms at the junction point of flowing water and flowing lava.

There are many ways to arrange such a junction, but the simplest is shown in Figure 3.2. You could sink this arrangement one block further into the ground and avoid having to place the bordering blocks, but we're going to use this layout because it lifts the cobblestone above ground level where it can be pushed with pistons.

Spill a bucket of water on the far left. It will flow down over the lip into the two-block-deep hole and, due to the mechanics of the water flow model, will actually, and rather conveniently, stop right there.

Then spill a bucket of lava on the far right, forming the cobblestone that was shown in Figure 3.1.

Try mining the cobblestone, and you'll see it pop out and another block form within moments. Infinite cobblestone. Pretty easy, right?

Let's ramp this up a bit.

Place a standard piston so that it's facing the cobblestone. (You may need to scoop the lava into a bucket and then remove the formed cobblestone before placing the piston because it can be quite tricky to obtain the right angle for the piston with the cobblestone block in front.) Figure 3.3 shows the intended layout.

It's possible to build a BUD switch, as described in Chapter 2, "Automated Produce Farms," to detect the creation of the cobblestone block and then activate the piston to push it out. However, an easier way is available that introduces a new type of circuit we haven't looked at before: the repeater clock.

FIGURE 3.2   Cobbling together some cobblestone.

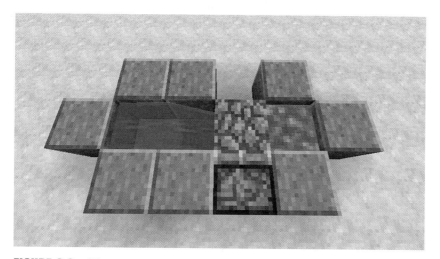

FIGURE 3.3   Pistons provide an easy way to push out a string up of up to 12 cobblestone blocks.

Clocks constantly repeat a redstone pulse. There are many ways to achieve this, including with the use of pistons, items moving between hoppers, and by just using a string of torch inverters. However, the easiest method for fine-tuning the interval between pulses is with a string of redstone repeaters arranged in a loop. In its default configuration, each repeater adds a 0.1 second delay to the circuit, with the slider on top of each repeater allowing this to be lengthened to as much as 0.4 seconds.

Figure 3.4 shows the circuit we'll use here. The pulse originates with the button attached to the plank block. A trail of redstone leads directly to the base of the piston, but also splits off into the repeater loop. As it travels through each repeater, it is ever so slightly delayed, eventually traveling around the entire loop in a clockwise direction, back through the plank block and toward the piston once more, and also restarting its endless circuit of the loop.

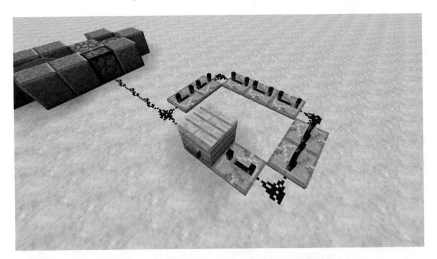

FIGURE 3.4 Clocking on and off with a repeater loop.

Create the circuit by laying the repeaters, ensuring they all run clockwise. Run the redstone to the piston and also to connect the repeaters; then press the button.

Now take a look at the piston. You'll see it start to push out the cobblestone, but there's a slight problem. The piston flies back and forth so fast that it spends most of its time blocking the flow of lava, preventing the cobblestone from forming. There's an easy way to fix this. Start right-clicking the repeaters, shifting their sliders back to the last available position. As you do so, the pulses will slow down. Keep going until you have the piston synchronized with the cobblestone production. I've found this requires setting six of the repeaters to their slowest position.

This is all well and good. You should see a row of cobblestone form, as shown in Figure 3.5, spanning out 12 blocks—the maximum a piston can push at any time. Try digging out any of those blocks, and the piston will quickly "heal" the gap with a new block of cobblestone. This is quite commonly used to create self-healing bridges, but why stop there? Let's create an entire self-healing platform—perfect for that game of Spleef (see the note "Playing Spleef") or just developing an expanse of easily minable cobblestone.

Start by laying down a line of pistons and blocks behind, as shown in Figure 3.6. Connect them up to the timing loop with some redstone. You'll also need to place one more repeater before the pistons to boost the current so they all fire off. Otherwise, the redstone trail will be a little long and will lose its punch before it reaches the end of the pistons. Other than that, that's all there is to it. If you need the platform created in a more specific shape, use other blocks that pistons can't shift to form the outline. This includes growing trees, other extended pistons, and most block-sized items such as dispensers, hoppers, furnaces, and the like.

FIGURE 3.5 Periodic pistons provide an easy way to push up to 12 cobblestone blocks out of the generator.

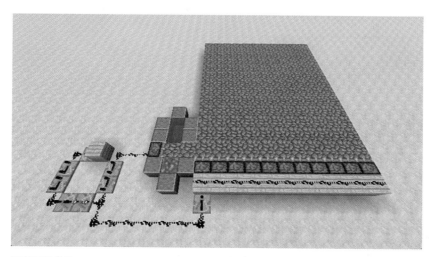

FIGURE 3.6 Creating a full self-generating platform—perfect for that game of Spleef.

NOTE

Playing Spleef

Spleef is one of the older arena games played in *Minecraft*. It can be played in a "vanilla" (or standard) *Minecraft* world without requiring a special server configuration. Spleef is played on a one-block-thick suspended platform. The idea is simple enough: Try to knock out the block under your opponent so they tumble into a deadly pit, lava pool, or other dastardly trap. The last man standing takes home the prize. There are numerous variations on the theme. As the game continues, the platform gradually turns into Swiss cheese, making just moving around something of a challenge. Arm the players with a bow and arrows, and the rapid movement required to dodge those fletched missiles turns the game into a rather joyful combination of parkour and abject hilarity. Playing with more than two people also adds to the frantic nature of the battle, and you can then become a little more creative, perhaps adding further platforms below so the battle can take place over multiple rounds, and throwing in some hostile mobs, protective barriers, and so on, to make things a little more interesting. Use a self-generating platform with a lever before the piston range to turn off the pistons while a match is in progress. The first line of blocks will still update, but another lever can solve that, or even a more sophisticated circuit that can switch them both off at once. Figure 3.7 shows a design that works off an AND circuit that is mirrored to accept two inputs from each end of the repeater loop, and a lever in the middle that acts as the master toggle. Remember to place the two redstone torches on the back end against the faces of their blocks.

FIGURE 3.7 This double AND gate controls two circuits with one lever.

Creating Stone

Stone appears abundantly in the Overworld and is also formed ad hoc when lava flows on top of still or moving water. When mined with a normal pickaxe, it turns into cobblestone. Because this takes less time to mine than cobblestone, stone generators are a slightly more efficient method of obtaining cobblestone than through an actual cobblestone generator. Stone mined with a pickaxe enchanted with Silk Touch will drop a stone block instead of cobblestone, but all is not lost if you're lacking one of these. Smelting cobblestone in a furnace also delivers a smooth, elegant stone block. Although using stone for construction, rather than the comparatively knobbly cobbles, is just a matter of aesthetics, it's nice to have the choice of either that a stone generator delivers.

Start by creating the layout shown in Figure 3.8. This is similar to the cobblestone generator with some subtle differences; in particular, take note of the position of the hole in the ground and the slightly different geometry of the border blocks.

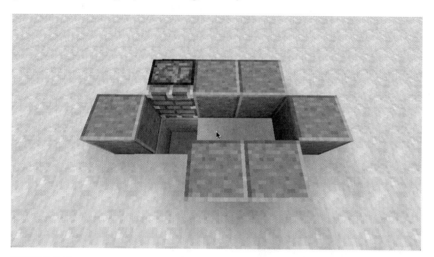

FIGURE 3.8 The foundation of a stone generator.

Now place a set of four glass blocks on top (see Figure 3.9). These act as the tower well for the lava, allowing it to drop down onto the flowing water. You'll need to add some temporary blocks to attach the two floating blocks in the correct position and then remove them. Alternatively, just create a square using eight glass blocks. Either way will work, and you can use any solid block material you prefer, except wood, which has the habit of bursting into flames when in close proximity to lava.

Finally, in this order, spill water into the far end of the trench and pour lava against the inside of one of the blocks at the top of the tower well. This positions the lava source block at the top of the tower so that it continually flows down. Assuming all has gone to plan, you'll see a block of stone form almost immediately under the lava (see Figure 3.10).

FIGURE 3.9   Creating a tower well for the lava.

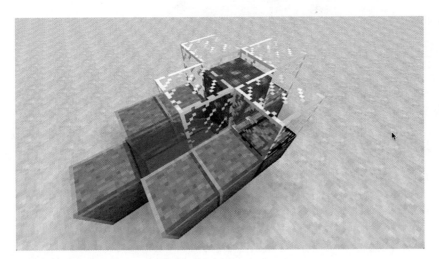

FIGURE 3.10   Place the water source first, and then the lava to ensure they meet in the correct order, forming stone.

All that remains is to set up the same circuit to control the piston as you used in the cobblestone generator. Just make sure you use a stone button on the circuit's starting block because stone buttons produce a 1-second pulse of power. A wooden button will push the piston forward for 1.5 seconds and not leave enough time while retracted for the lava to flow down once more into the water.

Extend the design further, if you like, by adding the same string of pistons shown in Figure 3.6 that created the self-healing cobblestone platform.

Obsidian Generator

Besides building portals, obsidian is primarily useful as an incredibly effective blast-resistant building material. I mentioned earlier that it is some 200 times tougher than any other, excluding the unmineable bedrock, and it is therefore also immune to the attacks of any naturally spawned hostile mob, including exploding creepers. Indeed, the only mob that can break obsidian is the player-created Wither.

Unlike the previous two generators, there is a core problem with automatic obsidian generation: the requirement of lava source blocks. Although it's possible to build an infinite water source by emptying two buckets of water into the diagonally opposite ends of a 2×2 hole, the same cannot be said for lava. In essence, lava source blocks are a finite resource within any particular chunk, although given the practically infinite size of each *Minecraft* world (approximately 64,000,000×64,000,000 blocks in surface area), not to mention the enormous lava pools found in the Nether, lava, like any other resource, can be considered essentially infinite.

At this stage there are several ways to obtain obsidian:

- Pour water on top of the still lava that fills lava lakes. These are most commonly found below level 10 in the Overworld, and everywhere in the Nether, although they do appear on the surface, especially when you're playing a customized world using the "Good Luck" preset (see Figure 3.11).

- Pour lava into a mold, as shown in Figure 3.12, and then place water on top to form obsidian in the final desired shape. This has the advantage that you don't need to mine the obsidian with a diamond pickaxe, saving wear on your tools. Figures 3.13 to 3.16 show how to mold a Nether portal frame without mining any obsidian. It doesn't take long at all and therefore is actually a more efficient construction method than having to tunnel down to layer 12 to find diamonds.

- Obtain enough obsidian to build a portal (including molding a frame, as described earlier), craft a chest (or a couple of ender chests for even easier content transfers), and pack a diamond pickaxe and a couple of stacks of stone or cobblestone. Place a bed and take a nap at night to reset your spawn point, and then clamber through the portal to travel to the Nether. This creates a portal at your destination, automatically spawning the obsidian blocks required for the frame. Create some protection around the frame using the cobblestone so that you can take the time to knock the obsidian out of the destination frame, piece by piece, without worrying about ghasts flinging fireballs your way. When you've finished, place the chest and store everything you have therein—every last skerrick. Then jump into some lava, fall off a cliff, or die in some other convenient way. You'll respawn next to your bed. Head into the frame again. A new one will appear either at the same place as the original Nether frame or nearby. Take some care before you step out because they can appear over lava, or very close to cliff edges. Then hoist your pickaxe from the chest, take apart the obsidian frame, and repeat. When you have enough, collect everything from the chest and travel back through the frame to the Overworld.

TIP

Bringing Back Disappearing Chunks

Chunks are columns of blocks, 16×16 in surface area, and 256 rows high. Each *Minecraft* world is divided into these chunks. Each spawns and is loaded in its totality as you travel around the different regions. If you find chunks not rendering correctly, leaving odd gaps in the ground through which you can see tunnels, dungeons, and so on in other chunks, try changing your video settings so that the Render Distance is set to 16 chunks. You may find this too much of a slow-down for a low-powered computer, but if you have a recent model with an equivalent of an Intel i5 or i7 CPU, there's a good chance your chunk gaps will become a thing of the past.

FIGURE 3.11 Convert a portion of a lava lake into obsidian by pouring water on a non-lava block nearby so that it has the chance to flow over the lava.

FIGURE 3.12 Mold obsidian with the placement of surrounding blocks, then pour a bucket of lava into the gap in the middle.

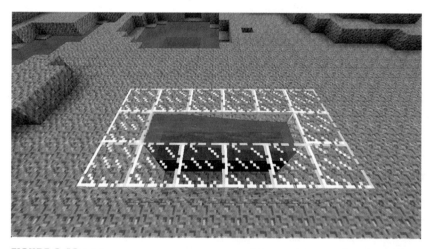

FIGURE 3.13 You can convert a row of lava with one bucket of water, but building a vertical tower requires a layered approach.

FIGURE 3.14 Build the frame one layer at a time, placing the lava and then water on top to control the conversion of the blocks. The left side of the frame is ready for the water, whereas the right side shows it already converted.

FIGURE 3.15 A final spill along a channel at the top completes the frame.

FIGURE 3.16 The frame is now ready for action and requires just 10 lava source blocks nearby if you leave out the corners.

The Bottom Line

Although you can't generate a huge number of the different ores in *Minecraft*, being able to create the basics, such as stone and cobblestone, can be a boon, saving you from having to tunnel through the countryside or mar the landscape with strip mines. Indeed, ever wonder how players create enormous structures while playing a game that is strictly Survival? Well, they don't do so by digging up all that ore. Generators take up very little space, and pistons are easy to create. Plant some saplings to provide wood for the handles, and you'll have all you need to build any number of pickaxes so you can keep pulling in the output from the generator and use it wherever you require. Build an enormous castle and turn the pistons so they face up and create towering walls. You may even want to use a generator to create huge platforms such as the one required for the mob farm described in the next chapter. Read on to gain a huge amount of other useful resources from mob drops.

Mob Farms, Traps, and Defense

In This Chapter

- Create mobs on demand.
- Gather a host of useful items and resources.
- Learn to build the best mob grinders.
- Create crafty traps.

Had enough of running around the countryside slaughtering hostile mobs just to get a few measly items? Ever fancied earning an unlimited number of experience points to use in enchanting? Take control of the mayhem with a mob farm: the equivalent of a factory for zombies, spiders, creepers, and skeletons. You'll quickly amass a fortune in useful resources, from gunpowder to string, arrows, and more, and also gather weapons, armor, iron, and even the occasional edible. Once you know how, it's really quite easy, and putting together a mob farm, especially when playing on Survival, is incredibly satisfying—not for the build, so much, but for the results. It will make a huge difference in giving you the resources you need to go crazy with TNT, quickly grow crops, provide countless arrows for long-range combat, and so much more. Mob farms that focus on the hostile game entities can deliver all of this and more (see Figure 4.1).

Evil Mob Farms

Mob farms are composed of two parts: spawning and grinding.

The spawner is usually a darkened room designed to encourage mobs to spring into existence and then wander or be driven to a central point that feeds into the grinder. The grinder kills the mobs outright or, through fall damage, harms them enough that they can be killed with a single blow, thus quickly accruing you experience points. Large-scale mob farms can spawn hundreds of mobs per minute, grind them up like so much raw meat, and deliver their drops through an automated collection system into a bundle of chests.

FIGURE 4.1 Mobs gathered at the base of a mob farm, ready to be attacked from a tunnel below.

Spawning Mob Mayhem

Because even the simplest spawner requires significant resources, it's best to plan it out carefully if you're playing on Survival. Keep the following points in mind:

- Mobs only spawn when the player is nearby, within an area of 240×240 blocks, so you'll need to be close to the farm for it to operate. There are ways to control spawning with mods, but I'll focus on the default behaviors here.

- Mobs can only spawn on opaque blocks, ruling out the use of glass platforms. This can make it difficult to see exactly what is happening inside a spawner unless you have cheats enabled and switch to Spectator mode by typing in the command **/gamemode spectator**.

- Hostile mobs only spawn at a light level of 7 or less, and the darker the better. (You can check the light level by turning on the debug screen. Press F3 on a PC; or fn+F3 on Mac OS X.)

- Slimes only spawn at levels below 40 above bedrock, although in swamp biomes they can spawn at levels 51 to 69. However, they also spawn very rarely and only then in certain chunks, so building a successful slime spawner can be quite haphazard.

- In an optimal configuration, up to 79 hostile mobs can spawn within a single potential area, but this represents the maximum amount available within the entire vertical section of the world. Therefore, a mob farm over an area filled with caves will not be as successful as one with fewer dark underground locations, unless you take the time first to light the caves so that they become invalid mob spawn locations, leaving only your own mob farm as the most viable location. You can also use Spectator mode, if you like, to check out the underground terrain, but it's a good idea to avoid it for a true survival experience.

- Building a mob farm in the sky, as described in the next section, will provide more flexibility, and you can wait at ground level for the drops, thus getting around the problem that mobs won't spawn if you're closer than 24 blocks to the spawning ground.

- Unless you specifically want them, and design for them, spiders can cause problems in spawners by blocking 1×1-wide channels. Dividing the spawning floor with raised blocks so that no flat area is larger than 2×2 will help prevent spiders from spawning, or you can just ensure there are no small channels that can cause them to block your spawner or grinder.

- Although there is no way to craft them, mob spawners exist in dungeons, abandoned mineshafts, and the Nether region. Leaving them in position and building a mob grinder around them can make it easy to create a farm that works for just the type of mob created by that spawner. You can increase the light level with torches to prevent the spawner from spitting out hostiles at you while you build and then reduce the level to kick it off.

TIP

Go Superflat for the Highest Spawn Rates

A superflat world doesn't have any caves, so it's an ideal place in which to test and compare different mob farm designs without them being affected by additional spawn points located underground. This will result in the maximum possible number of spawns during the day, when there are no other spawn locations available, providing for an easy comparison of different layouts.

The spawner designs fall into several general categories, although as with almost anything built in *Minecraft*, there are a myriad of variations on the theme. I'll show you the first:

- **Water based**—This is the most effective for the number of resources consumed, using streams of water to wash the mobs to a central 2×2 hole. The water can originate from a permanent source block, or, if you are feeling more sophisticated, from water dispensers containing buckets of water, controlled via redstone. The spawning area is two blocks high, allowing all the Overworld's hostile mobs to spawn, with the exception of Endermen, who teleport upon touching water.

- Piston based—A three-block-high spawning platform filled with corridors crisscrossed with trip wires to trigger pistons to push the mobs off the platform. This method also permits the spawning of Endermen.

Let's start with the mob farm and then build some grinders.

Building a Water-Based Mob Farm

The simplest design uses four water canals of eight blocks in length connected to a 2×2 hole in the middle of a platform. We're going to build this in the air, and use height to our advantage to create a fall grinder. I recommend you build this as a test in a superflat world set to Creative mode because doing so in Survival will take much longer due to the constant risk of dropping off your precarious perch. Follow these steps:

1. The first stage will look like what's shown in Figure 4.2. Start with a pillar 19 blocks high (see the note "Mob Fall Damage" for more information on why I'm not using the usual 22 blocks) and then build channels out from the pillar for the water flow that extend every direction for eight blocks. Each channel should be two blocks wide so that spiders can be successfully swept down to the center drop. You can use any material as long as it's opaque—generally speaking, that's any of the standard building materials except glass. Now block off the outside of each channel to contain the water and pour a total of eight water buckets against those blocks.

FIGURE 4.2   Water channels will sweep hostile mobs to their doom.

2. Lay an extra layer of cobblestone along the top of each channel, creating a watercourse that is two blocks deep so the mobs can't jump out after they've fallen in. Then connect that layer with a series of blocks along its circumference, as shown in Figure 4.3.

FIGURE 4.3   Adding to the mob farm's frame.

3. Fill in each of the four large spaces to create the spawning floor; then add a wall three blocks high around the edge, as shown in Figure 4.4.

FIGURE 4.4   The farm is now taking shape.

4. Finally, fill in the entire roof at the third level of the external wall, providing a spawning space two blocks high. Place some torches on top to prevent rooftop spawns that would sap from the total possible spawns, and feel free to remove the original support column (see Figure 4.5). Wait for daylight, or type **/time set day**, and you'll start to see a constant stream of falling mobs after 20 or so seconds.

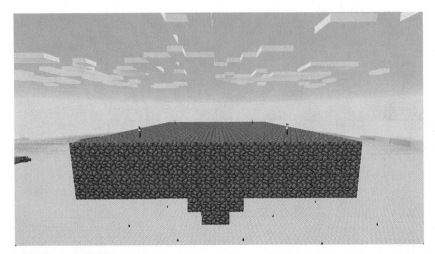

FIGURE 4.5   The finished farm: a mob spawner floating in the sky.

NOTE

Mob Fall Damage

Different species of mobs have varying amounts of health, so you can, in effect, choose which categories to kill and which to keep for later slaughter, and the subsequent experience points, according to their type. You'll also often gain more types of drops by dealing the final blow, including armor, iron, potions, weapons, and tools. The goal is to reduce the mobs to a single point of health, allowing them to be dispatched with a single punch. Spiders are the weakest at just 18 points, requiring a fall of 20 blocks to be left at death's door. Skeletons, zombies, and creepers all have 20 points of health, and need a fall of 22 blocks. Witches are the strongest with 28 points of health, requiring a fall of 30 blocks to reduce them to one point of health. You can either position your mob farm at the right level to achieve the types of direct kills you want or, as you'll see in the example here, use a pit dug into the ground to increase the drop and make it easier to adjust the specific kills. You can also change the ratio of survivals to direct kills from falls by adding a block or two to the pit to raise part of its level, permitting more survivors, even though they still have very low health. You can use this method to adjust the kill-versus-survivability ratio until you have found a happy medium between gaining automatic drops and the experience and additional drops afforded by dealing the final blow from the safety of your access tunnel.

Grinding Mobs and Collecting Drops

Now that we have a mob spawner, it's time to automate the grinding of the mobs and the collection of their drops.

There are several ways to deal with the mobs in a so-called grinder:

- **Fatal falls**—Drop them from a sufficient height and they'll splat on the ground, instantly dying and dropping any goods they carry. Alternatively, as I'll show later, you can drop them onto hoppers that lead to a chest, ensuring the automatic collection of drops. You can also set the height just right so that quite a few mobs survive, ready to be slaughtered with a one-punch hit so you can quickly gather experience points.

- **Lava blades**—Wash them downstream toward a sliver of lava propped up at head height so that the lava kills the mob without destroying its items. Collect the drops in a hopper and chest.

- **Suffocation**—Use pistons to push opaque blocks into the mobs, suffocating them to death.

- **Drowning**—Use water to trap the mobs in an area with no air pockets, causing them to die and drop their items.

I'll show you ways to build all four.

Collecting drops from a fall helps avoid the problem shown in Figure 4.6: a mass of item drops that will despawn if not collected in five minutes. (Items do persist if that chunk is unloaded from memory, which can occur if you travel a substantial distance away.)

FIGURE 4.6 Automatically collecting items provides a safe way to ensure they don't despawn.

Hoppers, whether stationary or attached to a minecart, can sweep up dropped items, so there are two ways to organize the collection:

- **Standard hopper**—Arrange hoppers under the kill zone of your mob farm, each feeding into the next like a line of pipes until the dropped items finally make it to a chest. Start by placing the chest; then Shift-click to arrange the hopper pipelines, building out from the chest, with each hopper feeding into the one adjacent. You'll need a substantial grid of hoppers, similar to that shown in Figure 4.7, which makes this a very costly setup on Survival because each hopper requires five iron ingots and one chest. If iron is in short supply, but you do have the six gold ingots required to create a set of powered rails, consider the next solution instead.

- **Minecart with hopper**—Set up a snaking rail line such as the one shown in Figure 4.8 using a minecart with hopper to scoop fallen items off the track. This works best if you have arranged the fall so that all mobs die when they hit the ground, because surviving mobs will block the movement of the minecart. Alternatively, use the lava blade to slice and dice the mobs so that you can be certain only items drop to the track. Although not shown, you can of course easily add a minecart unloading station (see Chapter 3, "Mining and Ore Generators") to this layout at one end, so that the hopper is periodically emptied. You can use another hopper to transfer the contents to a chest, or directly into another minecart with a chest that will haul everything back to base.

FIGURE 4.7   Hopping to it with a hopper grid to funnel drops from the kill zone into a chest.

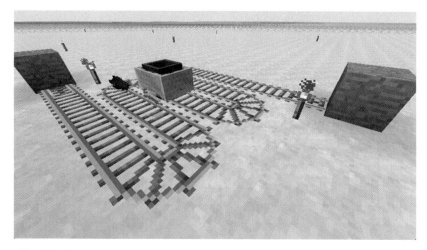

FIGURE 4.8 A single minecart with hopper and a snaking track can replace the hopper grid and is much less costly in resources.

Creating the lava blade requires some careful construction because you are, of course, dealing with lava, and you've probably already had that feeling of once burned, twice shy. Figure 4.9 shows the end result perched under the mob farm, but I'll take you through it step by step, starting at ground level as a proof of concept:

1. Start with a two-block-wide water channel, eight blocks long, as shown in Figure 4.10, with walls two blocks high to provide sufficient height for passage of the mobs. In practice, you can get by with a channel not quite so long, but you may find some mobs glitching through, in particular witches whose high health may help them survive the initial lava burn. You should position the channel so that the four blocks of water starting at the source are positioned directly under the 2×2 exit from the mob farm.

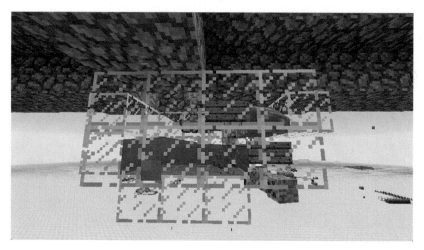

FIGURE 4.9 The lava blade is a simple, effective mob grinder.

FIGURE 4.10 The water channel feeds mobs to the lava blade.

2. Referring to Figure 4.11, extend the walls of the channel a further four blocks, and place two signs or ladder segments immediately after the water flow ends. These will hold up the lava, creating the "blade" effect. It's optional to have the second wall block on top of these sign blocks, hence the gap you can see in the walls. The lava needs to be positioned one block higher than the water, so also lay a further six blocks in the base of the lava channel as shown. (Note: I've also dug a 2×1 hole two blocks deep beneath the signs and positioned a chest. A couple of hoppers on top can feed all the drops into the chest, showing what will be a very compact version of a collection system.)

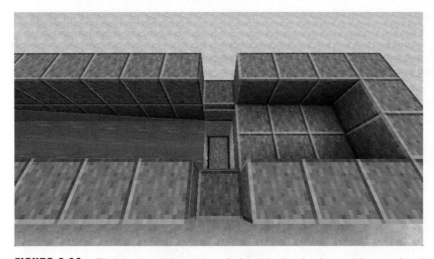

FIGURE 4.11 Finish the lava side of the blade design with a raised channel and signs or ladders to hold up the end of the lava flow.

3. Spill two buckets of lava at the far end of the lava channel so they flow toward the middle. You can see the final result in Figure 4.12 and the lava blade in action in Figure 4.13. If you've added the chest and hoppers, just dig an access tunnel in from the side to get to the chest's contents. In Creative mode, use the spawn eggs from the inventory window to add mobs to the grinder—strictly for testing purposes of course.

FIGURE 4.12   The final grinder. You may be able to spot the two hoppers at the end of the water channel, under the lava, that will direct any drops into the chest.

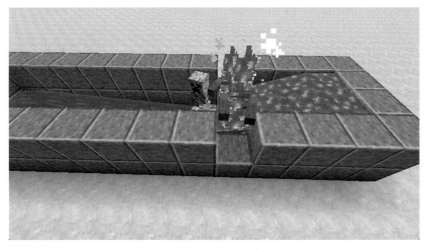

FIGURE 4.13   The finished lava blade, processing away.

By the way, this type of lava blade is the most resource efficient, but if you build four more signs, you can also significantly reduce the footprint by cradling the lava between them. Follow these steps to build this design under the mob farm:

1. Start by attaching blocks to the underside of the mob farm in the pattern shown in Figure 4.14. I'm using glass for clarity, but you may prefer to use an opaque block so that the grinder helps prevent light seeping into the mob farm from below. Attach the two signs to the inside walls of the blocks. If you are using an opaque block, you can also use ladders instead of signs. (Attaching the grinder to the mob farm can be tricky in Survival—build a sizable platform underneath that hangs off the original pillar so you can build in safety.)

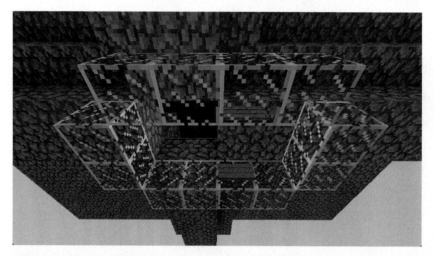

FIGURE 4.14 Adding the first layer of the lava grinder to the bottom of the farm. Don't forget the signs!

2. Now add a second layer of blocks in the shape of a U, with the opening at the end where the lava will be. Figure 4.15 shows the result.

3. Place a further six blocks one level down to fill in the base of the opening, starting under the farm's outlet and then continuing three blocks until the base has extended under the first of the signs (see Figure 4.16).

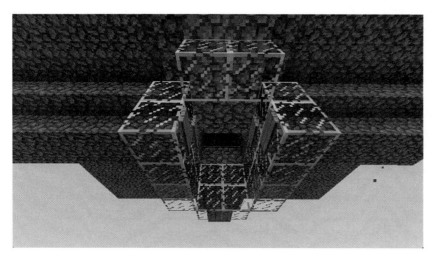

FIGURE 4.15 Completing the initial shape for the mob grinder.

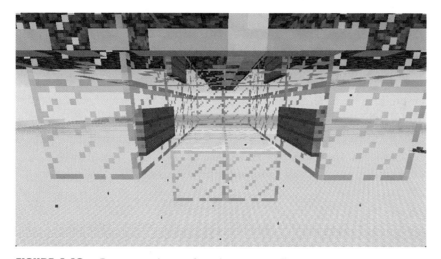

FIGURE 4.16 Create a base for the water flow.

4. Finally, move to the opening between the signs and place two buckets of water against the wall at the far end of the funnel so they originate under the farm's outlet. Then point your crosshairs at one of the side blocks nestled between the upper and lower signs, back at the lava end, and place a lava source block (see Figure 4.17).

FIGURE 4.17 Pour water at the far end of the tunnel, and lava at the near end, between the signs.

You should now have the same grinder as was shown in Figure 4.9.

By the way, trying to reduce the design even further by, for example, just placing a suspended pool of lava under the grinder outlet through which mobs can drop and catch fire on the way down won't actually work because they'll attempt to swim up in lava, causing all their items to also burn. The water moves them toward the lava where they can't swim up due to the block above their head, but items nonetheless can drop out below.

One final tip: This design, although extremely compact, does have an issue with light from the lava leaking into the mob farm, somewhat reducing its spawn rate. You can solve this by extending the water course, even as far as a full eight blocks, so that the lava is set much further back from the farm's opening.

Before we leave mob grinders, or at least start to look at them in the context of defensive traps, I want to show you one more technique that provides a safe way to collect experience points. Going back to the hopper layout from earlier, dig out a channel two blocks deep around the hoppers, and place two water sources on either side of the chest. These will flow around the 12-hopper grid and meet on the other side, sweeping any mobs that do survive the drop toward a central point, as shown in Figure 4.18.

Dig a single block out of the wall at the level of the water flow. (Or, if you are certain your drop is large enough that spiders can't survive, make it two wide.) Both streams of water are already at their eight-block limit for flow, so they won't fill the hole. Now dig an access path from above that leads to that removed block, finishing one block further down. This will allow you to attack any mobs that survive the fall, but they won't attack you back because you are at the level of their knees, as shown in Figure 4.19. Their drops will also collect in the water stream. You can gather these automatically by adding hoppers under the blocks at the end of the stream, one connected to the other, and then placing a double chest underneath them.

CAUTION

Look Out for Chicken Jockeys

The Chicken Jockey, usually a baby zombie riding on the back of a chicken, is a relatively recent addition to *Minecraft*, first appearing in v1.7. It's a rare spawn, but adds some danger to a mob farm where falls are used to deliver damage to the mobs. The chicken acts as the baby zombie's feathered friend, flapping its wings and preventing fall damage. These unusual mobs can also run through a one-block-high space, making them a danger when you're attacking mobs at leg height. You can ameliorate this by using slabs to create a half-block space through which you will still be able to attack mobs, but be safe from any crazed chickens trying to establish a new pecking order.

FIGURE 4.18   Add water flows around the hopper to sweep surviving mobs to your knee-knobbling access point.

FIGURE 4.19   This is, perhaps, an unfair way to gain experience points, but it certainly is a fast way to go about it.

Dastardly Mob Traps

There are numerous ways to build mob traps in *Minecraft*, many with very cunning designs. Indeed, the fall and lava grinders described earlier are two variants of this. However, think of a mob trap as being a defensive measure typically built up around your base. As with the grinders, they fall into the categories of those that seek to keep your base free of hostiles either by killing them outright or by corralling them somewhere for later killing at your leisure. You can use these other traps as replacement grinders, but they are primarily designed as a defensive measure. In fact, cactus is probably the closest *Minecraft* gets to a real-world tank trap!

Treacherous Trenches

The humble trench, two blocks deep, acts as one of the simplest mob traps available for creepers, skeletons, and zombies. A flow of water sweeps them down, or a river of lava can burn them up. Build some trenches around the perimeter of your dwelling, making them two blocks wide to also catch spiders, then add a transparent block on the inside top wall to prevent spiders climbing out and you should be able to go about your business without too much worry. You can add onto this by sweeping them into a lava blade. Build a compact version with a second stream to collect the drops as follows:

1. Dig a perimeter trench at least two blocks deep and two blocks wide, although if you need to spill water more than eight blocks around your perimeter, you will need to ensure the water level drops no more than every seven blocks, so the grinder will end up deeper than that shown in Figure 4.20.

2. Use the same approach as that for the farm, but use a V-shaped layout of signs or ladders to hold the lava in place, positioned one block above the end of the water.

You can get by with a single lava bucket, although I've used two because I prefer the aesthetics of a still pool of lava rather than one flowing from one position to the next.

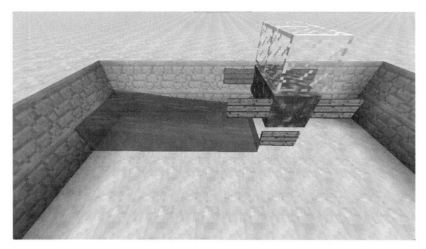

FIGURE 4.20 A short version of the initial watercourse. You can, of course, extend it as far as you need, around corners and so on.

3. Position any kind of block on top of the lava to keep the mobs from trying to swim up the lava and thus burning their drops.

4. Now, as shown in Figure 4.21, dig an outlet trench one block below the lowest part of the V and extend it to the right. If you just plan to pick up drops as you go, it can be any length, but you can also collect the drops in hoppers by placing the hoppers below the level of a very truncated stream. You should be able to make out two hoppers under the water in the figure.

FIGURE 4.21 Although guarding the perimeter is always worthwhile, it makes sense to also collect any drops rather than letting them go to waste.

If lava is in short supply, you can also use water blocks placed in the V pattern, as shown in Figure 4.22, to create a drowning pit. It will take longer for the mobs to expire, but given that an endless supply of water can be created by dropping just two buckets' worth into the diagonally opposite corners of a 2×2 one-deep hole in the ground, this type of mob trap is incredibly efficient.

FIGURE 4.22 Save some trips to the lava pool by using water instead. It's a little more painful on the ears because the mobs take longer to drown, but it's just as effective in the long run.

Killer Cactus

The cactus is a prickly customer. It's easy enough to grow, but if any mobs or players touch its side, they'll immediately suffer half a heart (or one health point) of damage. This makes it one of the easiest-to-use elements in many types of traps. The only downside is that a cactus also destroys some of the items that are dropped, so it's inefficient as a harvester for mob farms, but works just fine as a defensive strategy. The mob that gets swept into a cactus trap suffers a death of a thousand cuts, and although one wouldn't wish this on anybody, the cactus does make for a very space-efficient grinder, with the advantage that there are at least some collectibles at the end.

Figure 4.23 shows the most elemental of cactus traps. Any mobs flowing into the water are swept toward the cactus, where they'll bump up and down. The cactus should be at least two blocks tall to prevent mobs jumping over the top. A hopper in front of the cactus collects their drops, although, as mentioned, some items are destroyed in the process.

A cactus only grows on sand, so ensure you position that before you place the cactus. It also requires a transparent block on all four sides (air, water, or even lava will suffice).

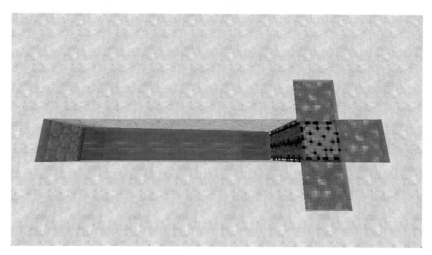

FIGURE 4.23   A basic cactus trap with a hopper to collect drops. Although not required, I've backfilled the three spaces around the cactus with lava.

Trapping spiders in a channel two blocks wide requires a minor change. The space requirements for cacti forces them to be placed diagonally, as shown in Figure 4.24.

There are numerous potential designs. A pool 4×4 across, as shown in Figure 4.25, with two cactus in the middle, a couple of hoppers adjacent, and four buckets of lava poured into each corner will sweep any hapless mobs to the center and drop their items into the hoppers. You can use feeder streams to feed the mobs into the pool, or just let them fall in from the top.

FIGURE 4.24   A cactus-based spider grinder requires a diagonal pattern.

FIGURE 4.25 A cactus pool with hoppers to collect drops.

Switching to the real world, you might consider using the natural fall of terrain to create a lengthier sequence, as shown in Figure 4.26. Any mobs that stumble in are inexorably swept downstream, bouncing off the cactus as they go. This isn't the most efficient design because mobs that drop in part way down will survive, but it's a useful example. You could, of course, finish them off with a lava blade or drowner, but you could also run some water down to the drowner without the cactus in place. However, this type of design is useful even without water as a simple, thorny mob trap. The mobs will wander up and down, taking constant hits as they go, and will eventually just keel over. Planting cacti in any type of trench will therefore clear out mobs over time—simple, effective, and deadly.

FIGURE 4.26 Using the terrain to flow water down through the trap saves digging a deep trench, and can deliver up item drops at the end.

TIP

Spider Spawners and Cactus

Spider spawners are an occupational hazard to anyone exploring abandoned mineshafts, dungeons, and the like. If you find one, consider partially blocking the entrance to the spawning room with cacti. Place a cactus on either side of the entrance, leaving just a single space between, and the spiders will rough themselves up against the cacti trying to reach you, until they eventually give up their lives and their string. Rig up a redstone lamp inside connected to a lever on the outside so you can trip the spawner into a dormant state and collect the string.

Indispensible Dispensers

The dispenser is a highly malleable key to many types of traps and defensive systems. It's easy enough to craft, requiring just seven cobblestone, a bow, and one piece of redstone, so making a lot of them probably won't strain the resource budget. The most difficult part may be collecting the string (three pieces for each dispenser to create each bow), but this can quickly be acquired with a mob farm.

Although dispensers require a redstone pulse to fire, the wiring is simplified compared to pistons and other devices. Instead of you having to feed the pulse directly into the dispenser, any pulse running one block nearby will prove sufficient. This means you can line up a string of dispensers and fire them all at once simply by running one strand of redstone behind, at the same level as the top of the dispenser, making it easy to create a wall of defense or offense, depending on your needs.

NOTE

Deadly Droppers? Not So Much

Droppers have their uses, in particular for quickly delivering items into your inventory, and they are the only tool in *Minecraft* that can transport items up vertically. However, because they drop the actual item entity itself, the same as if you have pressed **Q** to drop a held item, they are not much good for traps.

Dispensers have multiple uses:

- **Arrows**—Load a dispenser with arrows and it will fling a veritable fusillade with an almost 100% success rate if the mob is within one to five blocks. Unlike arrows fired by skeletons, you can pick up any arrows that miss their mark and hit the ground or embed themselves in other blocks, the same way you can for arrows you've fired yourself. However, you do have to pick them up yourself—you can't flush them down to a collection point with water. Shoot the arrows through a block of lava to turn them into flaming arrows that will set mobs on fire, causing even more damage. Take a look at Figure 4.27. The pressure plates are crafted from stone—don't use wood because the fired arrows will force the plates on continuously—and create a redstone current while the mob is alive. The clock circuit to the right keeps a continuous pulse running that hits the other side of the AND gate so that when the pressure plates are fired, a pulse flows to the dispenser, which shoots arrows through the suspended lava. Allow the lava to flow into a one-block hole below the level of the pressure plates so it doesn't spread down the tunnel. The stone button beside the clock circuit kicks off the first pulse and can be removed later. You can improve on this design by also adding a piston to the entryway of the corridor to block it off until the mobs have passed on. This will ensure the knock back from the arrows doesn't simply push them back out of harm's way.

- **Water and lava**—Create a cascade of water, or burning hot lava by placing the appropriate buckets inside the dispenser. As you probably know from Chapter 2, "Automated Produce Farms," dispensers place the liquid's source block in front of their outlet on their first trigger and then suck that source block back in again on the second trigger. The water or lava follows all the usual rules regarding flow.

- **Fireballs**—Firing a string of sizzling fireballs is a little extreme in Survival mode because they're quite expensive to make, but if you have the gun powder, blaze powder from defeated Blaze mobs, coal or charcoal, and the inclination, you can load a dispenser with a stack of fire charges and let fly. Interestingly, fire charges, like arrows, can be fired off just as successfully from a dispenser located under or behind water.

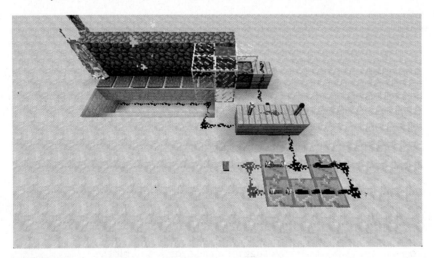

FIGURE 4.27   An automatic flaming arrow dispenser. (Front wall of tunnel removed for clarity.)

- **Spawn eggs**—If you are creating an adventure map, or in any other way using Creative mode, you can place mob spawn eggs in a dispenser and produce any of *Minecraft*'s mobs on demand. Want a player to trigger a wave of zombie attacks? No problem. Hit them with zombies, spiders, skeletons, ghasts, and so on.

- **Wall of flame**—I'm going to call this one "the toasty toes," and it's one of my favorite traps (see Figure 4.28). Place a flint and steel in an upward-facing dispenser and a pressure plate on an adjacent block, and the dispenser will shoot out flame, setting anything on top on fire. Remember to not use wooden fences near these traps because the fences will also go up in smoke, leaving you wide open. Stick to stone, although fence gates are, fortunately, fireproof. Flint and steel have a durability of 65 uses, so you may need to put several in each dispenser to ensure the longevity of this defense. Just remember to jump over the plate when you're coming back in—or create a single lane path between two dispensers; in almost all cases the mobs will still hit the plates as they wander around. If the worst happens on ingress, and you do catch on fire, just jump into a pool of water such as that shown in Figure 4.28 to instantly quell the flames.

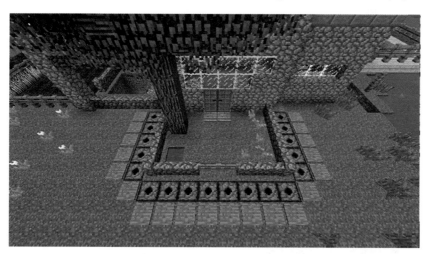

FIGURE 4.28 Overkill? Nah! Use upturned dispensers kitted out with flint, steel, and pressure plates to create the ultimate mob barbecue.

TIP

Refilling Dispensers

Dispensers emit a redstone signal through a comparator that reflects their inventory status. You could use this to automatically resupply them if they're running low on their projectiles. However, it is easier to just place a funnel on top of the dispenser with a chest above that. To successfully resupply a line of dispensers, you'll need to alternate the types of chests used so two singles don't combine into a single large double that feeds just the one hopper. Switch between standard and trapped chests to achieve the result shown in Figure 4.29.

TIP

Trapped Chests

Trapped chests provide something of a unique opportunity for creating traps that will fool other players—or, at least, noobs. They are almost indistinguishable from ordinary chests, except for a faint red tinge to the pattern that surrounds the latch, and placing a sign on the front with a suitably enticing message such as "Help yourself!" all but hides that from a furtively foraging adventurer. The chest emits a low redstone signal when open, so you'll almost certainly need to place a repeater against the back or sides of the chest to amplify that for travel of any distance, but that single-strength signal just happens to be, by fortuitous design, sufficient to explode a block of TNT placed directly behind.

FIGURE 4.29 Alternate standard and trapped chests to create a massive stock-pile of missiles on top of a line of justice-dealing dispensers.

Pulverizing Pistons

There's one other quite useful way to *process* errant mobs, both hostiles (except spiders) and players: the piston suffocation system. It's quite easy to make, and quick to complete its task. Figure 4.30 shows an example where, as we've done before, mobs are pushed down to the pressure plate by the water. The redstone torches act as an amplifier, providing a circuit that requires minimal space and resources, firing the piston as soon as the mob triggers the pressure plate. The glass block prevents the mob from escaping forward so that it is held in position until it dies and its items drop.

FIGURE 4.30   A basic mob suffocater using pistons and a pressure plate.

The only issue with this design is that it lacks a collection system for the item drops. They'll just sit on the pressure plate until they despawn or you stop by to pick them up. We can, however, improve on this. Figure 4.31 shows a modified design, this time with a hopper positioned where you'd expect—at the same level as the end of the water flow—and a pressure plate positioned on top. You can do this by Shift-clicking the hopper as you place the plate. (As an aside, it's possible to put all the other partial-height redstone items on top of hoppers: Plates, torches, repeaters, comparators, and daylight detectors all allow items to fall through into the hopper.)

A slight change to the wiring is required to detect the output from the pressure plate from an adjacent block, and space constraints require it to be set in front, with the output running back and into the torch under the block behind the piston. However, other than that, this improvement requires little more in the way of resources than the iron and chest required for the hopper.

FIGURE 4.31   Placing a hopper under the pressure plate allows hands-off collection of the mob drops.

One final note: Tripwire is an excellent way to trigger pistons, but like wooden pressure plates, it fires with both mobs and dropped items, so it requires a manual override to retract the pistons and permit collection of the drops. The easiest way to do this is with another AND gate, but this time using a lever in place of one of the redstone torches that acts as the override. Figure 4.32 shows an example. There is one glaring issue with the piston design: It's impossible to crush mobs that are just one block high because any piston placed on the same level as the tripwire or pressure plates will scrape them off as it pushes over the top.

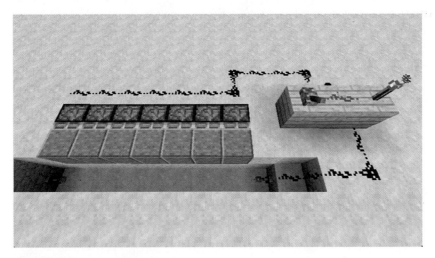

FIGURE 4.32   A tripwire and piston design using an AND gate to forcibly retract the pistons, providing access to any dropped items.

The Bottom Line

In this chapter, I've provided an overview of mob farms and various types of grinders and traps. As fits the ethos of *Minecraft*, there is no singular or *best* way to create any of these. In many cases you'll need to modify the designs to suit your own needs, and there are also numerous ways to combine, improve, and in other ways meld these to your specific requirements... or devious plans.

Speaking of which, when planning a mob farm, remember to explore the area underneath and light up any caves. It won't suffice to simply block them off. A deep ocean biome makes this easier because, whereas the ground beneath the ocean's floor can be as riddled with caves as anywhere else, there are no spawning areas within the parts actually filled with the wet stuff. This will increase the farm's spawning rate. However, mobs only spawn within a square area of 15×15 chunks, or 240 blocks per side, centered on the player, so you must stay fairly close to your farm for it to churn out mobs. On the other hand, mobs won't spawn at any location that is closer than 24 blocks in spherical distance from any player, so keep a polite distance to allow them to go about their spawning in private. If you have more than one *Minecraft* license and a spare PC, you could share a game on a LAN and position one player next to the farm to keep things ticking along while you do other things, and the same goes for when you're playing on other servers. Alternatively, install a mod such as Chicken Chunks that can keep chunks active at all times, no matter your own location. Download from http://www.chickenbones.craftsaddle.org.

Using mob farms and grinders is the single best way to gather enormous amounts of useful resources, so do delve in. You'll find them to be a constant reward.

Advanced Construction

In This Chapter

- Choose a building style that inspires you.
- Learn interior design tips to impress.
- Create natural-looking terrain and trees.
- Decorate with 2D pixel art.
- Build a 3D statue.
- Get cozy in the Nether and the End.

Building in *Minecraft* is not only wonderfully addictive, it's the perfect opportunity to unleash your creative genius. From a city of skyscrapers, luxury cruise ships, to perfect re-creations of your favorite film sets, *Minecraft* allows you to become, literally, the architect of your wildest dreams.

In survival mode, a lot of mining is required to gain all the necessary resources for a large build. If you're up to the challenge, then I recommend it—there's nothing more satisfying than creating a monumental build while pitted against the challenges of hostile mobs and declining health. Just remember to build scaffolding around your build to prevent your untimely demise. Creative mode is the best option if you are planning a big build because you'll have access to unlimited resources and easy (flying) access for high-builds and roofing (and screen captures!). Switch back into survival to enjoy your new abode once complete.

TIP

Think Outside the Square!

Although it's tempting to start with a rectangular floor plan and just build up, try to avoid it. Your house will look more authentic if it's asymmetrical (that is, your left and right sides aren't mirror images of each other). Use balconies, a split roof, covered walkways, sunken outdoor entertaining areas, gardens, and pillars to create a more inspired build.

Choosing a Building Style

Your building style is like your signature—uniquely you. The more you build, you'll find that certain techniques and tools suit you best.

If you are joining a multiplayer server, you may find there are specific rules attached to established cities that you must follow for your own build, such as a requirement to build your house in the style of the world, whether it be Medieval, Victorian, or Elvish.

In single-player mode, each world you generate will have a specific biome that may be suited to certain types of dwellings and artistry. In this section, we will look at each of the main building styles, along with the blocks and resources most suited to them and the most appropriate biomes to situate them in. (Note that this list is by no means exhaustive—for more ideas, trying performing a Google search for "architectural styles" and take screenshots of real-life buildings you can re-create.)

Medieval Style

Construction Elements: Castles, moats, hedge maze, watch tower, turrets, markets, taverns, swordsmith, and stables.

Complementary Building Materials: Cobblestone, oak, birch, mossy stone, glowstone, bookcases, iron, lapis lazuli, gold, and stone.

Complementary Decorations: Cauldrons, book and quill, enchantment table, potion brewing stand, mushrooms, furnace, redstone lamp, spider webs, and crops.

Arguably, medieval builds are one of the most popular, owing to the incredible scope for fantasy that *Minecraft* already entails—from potions to swords, armor, and dragon fighting. In this chapter, we'll use the medieval style as our main example (see Figure 5.1) to discuss construction in a little more detail.

Your first step in any large build is planning. Clear an area of land large enough for the build and then lay out the foundations of your house using colored blocks (see Figure 5.2). Mark the doorways, walls, and individual room layouts for your ground floor. Keep in mind your aspect (which direction you want your house to be facing) and try to make use of natural landmarks to incorporate into your build. Remember, it's better to dedicate time to planning now than to knock down walls later to resize.

FIGURE 5.1   Location, location, location—our cozy medieval castle overlooking the sea.

FIGURE 5.2   This medieval-styled home will be an ocean-view build with an upper-story deck, library, ballroom, a dungeon to house our Ender Portal and mine entrance, and a circular watchtower.

Up Go the Walls!

Because this build is multilevel with room to spare, our floor plan can be quite creative. Choose a primary color for your build and two or three complementary colors or textures to enhance your exterior. Carry those same tones inside for your carpets, wall art, and furniture.

Our medieval house example features a floor-to-ceiling bay window in the front ballroom to take advantage of the ocean views (see Figure 5.3). Your first story will usually include a living space and kitchen, amenities (bathrooms and toilet—superfluous, of course, but they add to the realism), and an entrance/ hallway. Plan your internal staircase position to take up the least space possible (unless it is a deliberately grand affair!), and use the space underneath for storage or dungeon access.

FIGURE 5.3 Get creative with your flooring—the floor is your largest canvas and is often overlooked. Experiment with colored wool blocks to create patterns, and dig a little to vary the height of your floors.

The ceiling of your first level will become the flooring of your second, so go ahead and build your internal walls up, taking note of door and window positions. I recommend a minimum five-block-high ceiling to account for later interior design. Generally speaking, the higher the ceiling, the grander the house.

To keep with our medieval theme, a high tower is built next to our dungeon, fitted with an internal staircase (see Figure 5.4). This tower circle is based on a simple 8×8-block diameter. We'll be looking at building circles, spheres, and arches in more detail later in this chapter.

Your second (and higher) levels offer the bonus of deck space (see Figure 5.5). Remember to bolster them with supporting beams or arches, which, although not strictly necessary, add to the realism of your build. In our example, the second floor fireplace has been positioned over the first floor fireplace using Netherbricks and iron bars. Keep wood at least two blocks away or it could burn.

FIGURE 5.4   A watchtower or turret is a medieval standard and adds an interesting contour to your build. Make sure it is properly lit with safe internal stairs to the top to avoid a fall at night.

FIGURE 5.5   The second story floor plan usually accommodates bedrooms, bathrooms, library/study areas, and specialty rooms.

If You Like It, Put a Roof on It!

As simple or complex as you make it, the roof will be the standout feature of your build. Roofing styles vary depending on your build (domed, pitched, complex, arched, flat, and so on); however, we'll cover a few of the main types in this chapter. The most common roof style you'll use is a simple pitched roof (see Victorian style, next). To create the diagonally attached rooflines you'll be using most often, add a temporary supporting block to attach your required block to. Once your desired block is placed, knock out the supporting block and continue your row (see Figure 5.6). You'll be using this method a lot for general construction and will quickly become efficient at it.

FIGURE 5.6 Create diagonally attached rows of blocks using a temporary supporting block. I've just knocked out the one below. Thereafter you can attach blocks to the face of the first.

Remember that your roof is valuable real estate within your house. Make good use of your attic space within a pitched roof, and add conversation features such as circular towers, chimneys, roof gardens, lookout platforms, covered walkways, solar panels (daylight sensors or pressure plates), and swimming pools. In Figure 5.7, we have a top view of our finished medieval house, complete with a semicircle lookout deck, covered walkway, glass-ceiling ballroom, and watchtower at the back.

FIGURE 5.7   Use different contours and stagger the floors up to the rooftop to add interest to the design.

Victorian Style

Construction Elements: Chandeliers, street lamps, pitched roof, landscaped gardens, elaborate rooflines with chimneys as well as bay windows and attic windows with decorative eaves

Complementary Building Materials: Stone bricks and wood primary blocks with richly colored feature blocks above and below the windows and door frames

Complementary Decorations: A neat garden box surrounding the trees, a park bench, and window boxes for flowers and shrubs.

Victorian-styled houses are an early 1900's ornate architectural style (see Figure 5.8). They generally feature a raised porch, large bay windows, and fairly symmetrical rooms. Begin with a square foundation but build high—two or three levels (see Figure 5.9).

There are two main types of Victorian roof styles. You'll find that these styles are also compatible with many other builds, particularly the pitched roof style. Therefore, we'll go into a bit more detail about roof construction here.

FIGURE 5.8   The key to Victorian builds is the fine detail, such as awnings above all windows and doors, internal architraves and balconies, and chandeliers and lamps.

FIGURE 5.9   Use a rich trim block to complement your brick, wood, or sandstone primary color.

Pitched Roof

The pitched roof is your go-to roof. It provides plenty of attic space and a nice triangular facade. Here are some points to keep in mind when creating one:

- Extend your roof frame at least one block past your external walls to add depth to your house.

- Step your roof blocks up to a center point across the front and back edges of your roofline.

- Create a feature point to your front and back facade—for example, an internal triangular shape beginning two-thirds across the length or an attic window with eaves. Overlay this line with stairs and remove your original pre-layer blocks (see Figure 5.10).

FIGURE 5.10   Use diagonally attached rows to extend your roof frame to full cover.

- Extend your horizontal roof blocks from front to back until they meet, and then overlay with stairs.

- Remove the pre-layer blocks from the facade on the front and back roof faces, back to wall level; then fill in your facade with a complementary colored roof block to surround your feature window.

- Use attic windows and small balconies as an opportunity to individualize your roof shape (see Figures 5.11 and 5.12).

FIGURE 5.11 Cover your attic window with its own A-frame awning to break up the empty space.

FIGURE 5.12 Try inset variations to add a decorative focal point. Keep the color scheme consistent with the front of the house.

Complex Roof

You can find some spectacular examples of complex Victorian rooflines online, providing plenty of inspiration for you. Here, I provide some tips for achieving an authentic look.

Complex rooflines are essentially the result of connecting multiple roof features together. Although tricky at first, with a bit of practice you'll create a masterpiece in no time.

- Extend your roof frame at least one block past your external walls to add depth to your house.

- Modify your roofline (and if possible your original house shape) to include interesting variations to the shape of your roof (for example, add a feature window, gables, a turret, or chimney). Use these variations in length of roof edges to create individual triangular peaks (using the standard step method) off your main roofline (see Figure 5.13). We will be following each of these smaller peak lines back into our roof and connecting them together.

FIGURE 5.13   Building variations into the shape of your floor plan gives you the opportunity to vary your roofline, too. Include sections of shorter wall, fireplace extrusions, and turrets to create smaller, individual peaks.

- In each place where multiple rooflines connect, add a corner block.

- Cover all your roof blocks with matching stairs, following the same lines. Just like with your pitched roof, you'll extend each row of roof blocks in turn—this time from the outside toward the center to their meeting points. Do it in sections, and try to keep your junctions at the same place for each level, thus producing a "step" effect as shown in Figure 5.14.

- On each of your smaller, "feature" roof shapes, remove the pre-block layers back to wall level so your decorative steps are more visible.

- The finished roof should have a very "stepped" appearance, meeting at the highest points (see Figure 5.15).

FIGURE 5.14 Cover completed block lines with steps that meet at the same points.

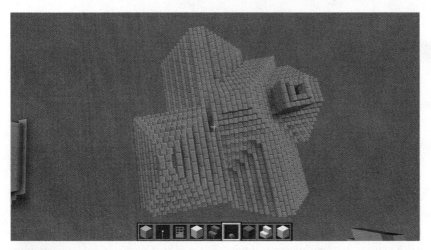

FIGURE 5.15 A complex roof takes a little practice but looks fantastic.

Japanese Style Building

Construction Elements: Simple, rectangular houses with a double overhanging roof. Cherry blossom trees using pink wool and birch logs. Miniature gardens with rock pools overhung with willow trees.

Complementary Building Materials: Cobblestone, white wool, dark logs, sugar cane, trap doors, and fence posts.

Complementary Decorations: Lily pads, hanging baskets, and lanterns.

Keep your buildings minimalist with dark wood poles and white wool walls. Traditional Japanese houses usually have rice paper sliding door, so a standard door should be replaced with either a trap door or other light-colored material for an authentic look (see Figure 5.16).

FIGURE 5.16 A rural Japanese house with double-layered roof and cherry blossom tree.

This style is deceptively tricky to accomplish, owing to the rather ornate roof. Follow these steps for a double-layered roof effect:

1. Use light-colored steps to frame the top of your wall and use a block to join each corner.

2. Extend the bottom step with a lowered, floating row of slabs. Place an additional slab on the corner diagonal to your corner blocks.

3. On the top of your roof blocks, use stairs pointing outward to add some height and, again, complete the corners with a slab.

4. Fill in your ceiling at the level of your original dark poles with a matching dark wood. Add another layer of slabs on top of your stair roof blocks; then extend these with another two rows of floating slabs to form a second canopy over the original roof (see Figure 5.17).

5. On top of your roof, add an internal rectangle of dark wood blocks, then light wood on top of this. From the outside, encase in another row of inward-pointing stairs down each length, creating the height for your pitched roof. Leave the front and back sides clear for your decorative fill.

6. Add two more sets of floating stairs to bring your roof to a point and fill the triangular front and back facings with dark wood and white wool. Add a row of slabs along the pitch seam to finish it off.

FIGURE 5.17 Slabs and inverted and upright stairs are the key to a multilayer roof.

Decorate your Japanese-styled house with decorative slabs, hanging lanterns, and willow trees with long, hanging leaves. You can also make cherry blossoms from pink wool. Landscape with rock gardens, complete with rock pools, lily pads, and stone benches. Keep the interior furnishings simple with smooth textures, and use sugar cane to imitate bamboo screens separating your living areas.

Modern and Suburban Styles

Construction Elements: Media room, swimming pool, Jacuzzi, garage, billiard table, garden roof, solar panels (daylight sensors or pressure plates), driveways, and an outdoor entertaining area with a barbeque or fire pit.

Complementary Building Materials: Ice windows (opaque), smooth colored clay or quartz to simulate rendered walls, and sand, water, and bamboo for external window screens. For a more suburban look, try red bricks, light wood panels, and colored wool in complementary colors.

Complementary Decorations: Bamboo, flower pots, glass and sandstone water features, cauldrons for sinks and toilet, horizontal window panes, and bushes in a jukebox planter.

The sky is the limit with modern-looking builds; simply take a walk around your neighborhood for inspiration—from ultra-modern concept homes (see Figure 5.18) to classic suburban sprawl (see Figure 5.19).

FIGURE 5.18   Smooth clay and quartz make a realistic "rendered" look.

FIGURE 5.19   A classic suburban brick home.

Keep the following points in mind when creating a modern-looking build:

- Smooth, clean lines with long horizontal windows add to your modern feel. Choose a light base color for your primary block, layered by a complementary feature block (either colored or textured) to highlight the main entrance and break the monotony of a space with a trim.

- Make good use of height. Dropping your hallway down a block or two after your entrance allows for higher ceilings in your living space, giving modern homes a spacious feel.

- Make good use of your roof space for gardens. Use bone meal on your gardens for super-fast growth (see Figure 5.20).

- Swimming pools add a great aesthetic element to the roof of a modern house; however, you'll need to create a double-block reinforcement base to overcome internal leaking.

- Multipurpose the space under your staircases for storage or continue them down to into a basement.

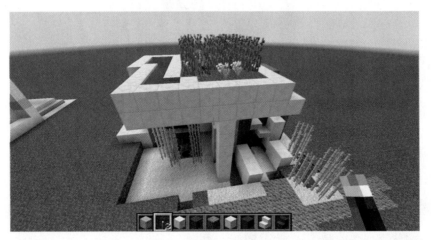

FIGURE 5.20   Utilize the space on your roof for solar panels, gardens, and water features—the perfect urban retreat.

Residential Roads

Use this pattern to create a road for your city or residential streets:

- One black wool
- One snow
- Three black wool
- One gold

Then repeat in reverse. Dig two blocks down so you can have one block higher for your sidewalk and one further step up to the grass level. Create your intermittent divider line as three gold blocks, then two black, three gold, and so forth (see Figure 5.21).

FIGURE 5.21 Take to the road and expand your horizons—why not build a city? Expand the number of lanes on either side of your divider to create a highway.

TIP

Give Your Exteriors Depth

Bring feature blocks, foundation pillars, and shaped walls out beyond your floor plan to create an interesting depth to your exterior. Extend roof blocks for an overhanging effect, and add garden boxes under your windows with shutters and eaves to draw attention to them. Remember, detail and depth are your friends—you'll take your build from ordinary to extraordinary with a little extra creativity.

Viking Style

Construction Elements: Very steep roof, curved in the middle with decorative end pieces. A cozy, practical interior with a large fireplace as the focal point. Create a split-level interior so you can overlook your living areas from a bedroom alcove above. A longhouse (communal living and eating halls) has wooden frames and stone foundations. A ritual house (similar to a church) is a simple wooden building displaying weapons of defeated enemies, often highly decorated on the roof and at the entrance.

Complementary Building Materials: Oak and spruce, logs and panels for buildings with stone foundations. Ice, snow, clay, sand, and white wool for contrasting patterns. Dark wood paneling inside and out will contrast with your snowy landscape.

Complementary Decorations: Snow, snow, and more snow! Spruce trees, flower boxes, and shrubs. For interior design, use decorative shields and patterned wall hangings in frames.

Building a Viking house is a fun challenge, given their very interesting rooflines and decorative pieces. The outside of the house should look a little dark and intimidating (see Figure 5.22), but the inside should resonate with warmth and shared space. Lay out your house foundations using dark logs outside a rectangular floor plan. Extend your walls (either double or single level) in a light color wool or timber to your roofline.

FIGURE 5.22 Home is where you lay your axe.

A Viking-style house is generally known for its very steep roof (to prevent the snow from piling up!) and the concave curve of the roof spine. Your roof will be long with a prominent single-length spine; however, if you're keen to individualize the rooflines in your Viking village, you can incorporate an additional roof feature using the same method as the complex Victorian roof, discussed previously.

Using partly overlapping roof blocks or slabs, gradually curve the spine of your roof to a peak at each end. The end result will look similar to the bow shape of a boat.

Decorate each end (and any high window eaves) with a tall decorative end piece to emphasize the height of the roof—usually made from a combination of inverted stairs and slabs (see Figure 5.23). Experiment with stairs, blocks, and slabs to find your perfect match—just keep it steep.

FIGURE 5.23   A Viking-styled roof is tall and thin with a decorative concave spine. In this example, the roof was made by diagonally connecting an inverted stair underneath an upright stair.

Egyptian/Desert Style

Construction Elements: Geometric designs, pyramids, tombs, statues, markets, temples, residential areas of geometrically shaped sandstone buildings close together (think horizontal Tetris on a grand scale), outlying wheat farms, and a single majestic water feature for royalty.

Complementary Building Materials: Sandstone, sand, orange wool, gold, glowstone, and clay.

Complementary Decorations: Cactus, sugar cane, parchment, and tomb offerings such as empty flowerpots for canopic jars, seeds, wheat, flowers, and rotten flesh (or mummified, in this case!)

There's nothing quite like the magnificence of a monolith. If you find yourself in a desert biome, make the most of it and turn the abundance of sand into something a pharaoh would kill for. Building a pyramid (see Figure 5.24) or temple is quite easy using our pitched roof technique (see Figure 5.25). If you're feeling a little more ambitious and want a sphinx to keep you company, consider experimenting with 3D modeling software (we'll get to that later in this chapter).

FIGURE 5.24   The majesty of an Egyptian pyramid is just the beginning. Take your build underground in a maze of tombs, tunnels, and redstone booby traps.

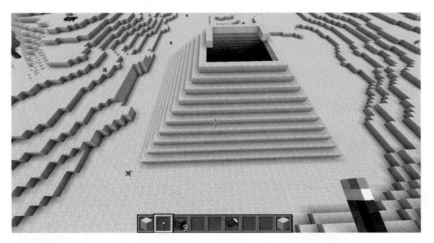

FIGURE 5.25   Use the pitched roof technique to layer your pyramid walls.

Steampunk Style

Construction Elements: Ships and steam-powered machines, Victorian-era buildings with dark, gothic decorations, airships, floating islands, crooked architecture, and wooden furniture.

Complementary Building Materials: Dark oak blocks, cobblestone, fence posts, iron bars, dispensers, posts and lanterns, steel, and colored wool.

Complementary Decorations: Robotic contraptions, levers, gears, misshapen furniture, spider webs, steel bars, wooden architraves, complex rooflines, and lots of internal stairs and cupboards.

Steampunk is an eclectic mix of old and new—combine modern ideas with old-fashioned technology and you can't go wrong. Mechanical objects should be steam powered and manually intensive, but with a whimsical element of fantasy behind the design. Figure 5.26 illustrates a 3D steampunk schematic imported from Minecraft-Schematics.com. Get online for some incredible builds in this style that will blow your mind.

FIGURE 5.26 This steampunk house and windmill 3D model imported from Minecraft-Schematics.com illustrates the fanciful style.

Elven/Fairy Style

Construction Elements: Tree houses, aerial walkways, glowstone lights hanging from trees, and waterfalls. Create a central meeting point (large waterfall/garden) surrounded by hanging leaf houses. Build spiral stairs within or outside the trunk of an enormous tree to create a multilayered tree house (see creating natural terrain and trees for more detail).

Complementary Building Materials: Moss stone, jungle leaves, jungle wood blocks, meandering paths made of cobblestone or intermittent sunken logs, ladders, and glowstone.

Complementary Decorations: Lily pads, sunflowers, vines, mushrooms, and spider webs. Create nature-worship sculptures to hide throughout your forest.

To create monstrous trees for your jungle tree house or fantasy theme, plant four jungle tree saplings in each block of a 2×2-block space. Make sure that all surrounding blocks are plain dirt and there are no obstacles within a radius as high as the sapling. Add bone meal to convert them to a large jungle tree of 2×2 blocks, complete with vines, instantly.

Clear some more blocks for dirt next to it, repeat the process and your tree will expand accordingly. If you're looking for epic height, create a "nest" in the top of your tree to lay another four dirt blocks (preferably hidden from view) and repeat the process.

Build an Igloo

If you've been dumped in the freezing grip of a snow biome, why not make the most of it and build an igloo to keep yourself safe and warm, like the one illustrated in Figure 5.27. If you're in creative mode, go ahead and use ice blocks to follow the basic pattern shown here. If you're in survival mode, you'll need to mold your ice and wait for each layer to freeze, which I detail in the following steps:

FIGURE 5.27 Fight off the winter chill in a redstone torch igloo.

1. Dig a circular pattern on the snowy ground. Keep in mind that each layer needs to freeze independently—bigger igloos take time.

2. Dig the center two blocks deep and then refill the bottom layer with the snow you removed. Fill the ground layer with glass blocks to prevent mobs spawning (see Figure 5.28).

3. Build a mold of dirt blocks on either side of your outer circle ring as a mold. Once in place, fill the inner core with water and wait for it to freeze.

4. You'll need a two- or three-block entrance (with snow and glass floor). Using the same "mold" method as before, create a dirt tunnel (in case you haven't guessed yet, the mold is temporary). Mold walls to your tunnel using dirt blocks one space further out and then block the end. Fill with water and let it freeze, as shown in Figure 5.29.

5. Repeat this process a number of times, giving your igloo some height. Just increase your mold each interval while the top-most layer of blocks are freezing.

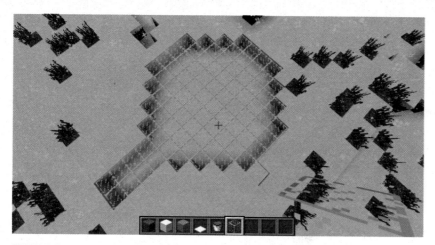

FIGURE 5.28 A glass floor will stop mobs spawning inside.

6. After a two-block-height tunnel has been frozen for your entrance, block off all external edges to create a tunnel ceiling and allow it to freeze. Your entrance tunnel should be lower than the igloo interior.

FIGURE 5.29 Use dirt blocks as a temporary mold while your water freezes.

7. Once you have achieved the wall height you desire, you need to create a dome. Cover your top ice ring with dirt blocks to create the external wall of your mold. Leave an internal block empty (for water) and create a second dirt-block ring as the internal wall of your mold. Fill with water.

8. Once frozen, repeat this process, bringing your water ring in consecutive layers inward, until you close off your ceiling using a small square on a base of dirt (see Figure 5.30).

FIGURE 5.30   Mold your layers inward to form a domed roof.

9. Once your roof has frozen, dig away all your dirt blocks, including the ice blocks blocking your entrance tunnel, leaving an ice shell.

10. Add a door to the inside of your entrance by replacing the floor block with snow. Decorate with redstone torches inside (don't build a fireplace!) and fit out with some home comforts.

Advanced Decoration Techniques

Designing your home, inside and out, is largely a matter of personal taste. However, do make sure that you are consistent throughout your build, using a set of complementary materials and colors that will carry through both your exterior features and decorative furniture.

Don't try to incorporate too many elements in a single structure—you'll end with a jumble-sale effect of mismatched colors and textures.

For example, door frames, eaves, and foundation pillars in a secondary color can be carried through to your fireplace, bedding, feature walls, and furniture for a consistent theme.

Generally speaking, a modern house will use smoother surfaces, spacious rooms, and clean lines; whereas dark, raw woods, cobblestone, and iron doors suit medieval- and rustic-style builds.

NOTE

Hundreds of incredible texture packs are available for download online to enhance your *Minecraft* builds. You can search these by category, resolution, and popularity to find the most suitable. Visit http://www.planetminecraft.com/resources/texture_packs/ to rummage through literally thousands of packs.

Here are some interior concepts to get you started:

Windows

- Use glass planes to create a pattern in glass block windows for detail without obscuring the view.
- Enhance your windows and doors with eaves, shutters, and sills to complement your primary block color.

Bathrooms

- Use a half-slab floor in the bathroom so your toilet and bath sit lower.
- To create a toilet, fill a cauldron with water and pop a hatch on the top for the open-close lid. A quartz block behind with a button on the top acts as a cistern.
- Try building an exact replica of your bathroom on the other side of your ice "mirror" panes to create a realistic reflection.

Walls

- Line your doors with the external wall for a more aesthetic house silhouette.
- Experiment with room dividers and internal walls to include shelves (inverted stairs), glass mosaic features, and split-pattern feature walls.
- Line the bottom row of your walls to base window height with a feature brick, log, or texture to liven up large areas.
- Sugar cane makes a bright, sophisticated room divider. Plant it in sand with an adjacent row of water as a feature point.

Flooring

- The topsides of pistons and furnaces make fantastic patterned floors.
- Use slabs to create a stepped flooring pattern, like Figure 5.31 from our medieval build library.
- Sandstone and Netherbrick create a stunning checkerboard combination—inside and out. (Giant garden chess, anyone?)
- Try using a leaf block in your flooring pattern for a neat look.

■ Sink crafting tables into the ground for a fantastic gothic-look floor.

FIGURE 5.31 Break up the monotony of floorboards with sunken slabs.

Kitchen

■ Pressure plates on top of your oven and crafting bench make a nifty kitchen counter.

■ Place a few redstone torches under pistons for a kitchen table.

■ To make a fridge, place a snow block with a side button on top of a dispenser filled with food (see Figure 5.32). Add an iron door to the front panels. Push the button and, voila, dinner time!

FIGURE 5.32 A dispenser in your fridge means fast food!

Furniture

- Place colored wool behind your chair backs to create cushions.
- Build your armchair around a minecart on a single powered rail for a chair you can actually sit in.
- Create a television by placing two black wool blocks on two bookshelves with a painting attached to one face. Add a lever to the top for an old-school antenna.
- Place a small painting on the front of a half slab with a pressure plate flat on the table in front, and you have a laptop ready for use!
- Build bunk beds by placing a bed on top of two rows of logs; remove the logs underneath and add a second bed in their place.
- A bookshelf base with a fence post holding a glowstone (add trapdoors to the sides) makes a soft glowing lounge lamp.
- Add a layer of carpet to the end of your bed as a throw.
- A layer of ice blocks surrounding plants with a wooden base and top make for an extravagant aquarium room divider.

Lighting

- Place an anvil in an item frame and then attach a torch (aim for the block behind) for a feature look.
- Use black wool walls to absorb light for deliberately dark rooms.
- For rooms with a six-plus-block-high ceiling, add a chandelier. Hang a glowstone block from a fence post mid-ceiling and place a torch on each face. Knock away the block and replace it to remove the connecting post arms (see Figure 5.33).

FIGURE 5.33 A chandelier adds elegance to the high ceiling of the ballroom.

External

- Create a boat dock behind your house and dig an underground river tunnel to the sea.

- Dot white wool from your chimney as smoke for that cozy, "lived-in" look.

- Use the chandelier technique to create a lamppost; simply overhang your light source from a tall post connected to a fence at the top.

- If your modern house boasts a swimming pool, use slabs to create a diving board.

- A hedge maze made of jungle leaf blocks is a fun addition to any medieval build—place a reward in the center for your guests!

- Create an ever-burning outdoor barbeque using flint and steel or fire-charges on Netherbrick over a cobblestone grill, surrounded by red bricks.

Creating Natural Terrain and Trees

If you're keen to make your build as natural and realistic as possible, you'll achieve the best effect by using your existing environment to your advantage. Build around it, using all the curves, imperfections, and oddities you come across as opportunities to individualize your home.

Of course, there are times when you seed into a super-flat world or wish to create a natural environment around an existing build.

Mods such as MC Edit (www.mcedit.net), WorldEdit (http://minecraft-mp.com/plugin/worldedit/) and VoxelSniper (http://dev.bukkit.org/bukkit-plugins/voxelsniper/) are powerful tools for creating large-scale changes in your environment. These are open-source software packages running on multiplayer servers online or available for offline single-player use, and are not associated with Mojang. (See Chapter 1, "Getting Started," for more on installing mods.)

Essentially, these programs have long-range mapping tools that allow you to make epic terraforming changes to your environment, in game. You can use different brush types to make detailed edits to individual blocks from a distance, or you can execute mass changes to grouped objects and place new objects. For example, one style of brush will build raised terrain such as mountains and hills, whereas another will "scoop" blocks (effectively replacing dirt with air) to create oceans, trenches, valleys, and canyons.

You can "naturalize" your new sculptures by typing a command to cover them in grass blocks, as well as place trees and natural objects on the surface. All programs also allow you to change all blocks within a connected mass (for example, a mountain of sand to dirt, or a valley floor from stone to clay). You simply set the radius of the brush to the size area of blocks you wish to convert per click.

Additional plug-ins and mods are available that will generate a forest around your house; however, sometimes the hands-on approach gives you more control over your environment. The most important thing to remember when creating natural terrain and trees by hand or mod is to lose the symmetry. Use unpredictable sizes and skewed shapes. Nature isn't perfect, and that's part of its charm.

Drawing 2D Pixel Art

Re-creating your favorite image in *Minecraft* is not too difficult; however, you'll need an image editor. Windows comes with the Paint program installed, which will suit your purposes. Alternatively, you can get free software from www.pixlr.com or www.getpaint.net or a 30-day Photoshop trial from www.adobe.com.

In the following example, we'll repaint a vintage classic, Astroboy, into our pixelated sky. To begin, load your image into the software. If the image has too many colors and details, convert it to a 16-bit format to minimize the colors (see Figure 5.34).

FIGURE 5.34   Load the image into the software.

Reduce the image size until your picture is pixelated to a point that will be easy for you to replicate using *Minecraft* blocks—one colored block per pixel. The larger the image size (and hence higher number of pixels), the longer the build will take. Next, lay gridlines over your image to easily differentiate between individual pixels (see Figure 5.35).

Finally, use this schematic to copy your image, line by line, into *Minecraft* using colored blocks that closest match your image colors (see Figure 5.36).

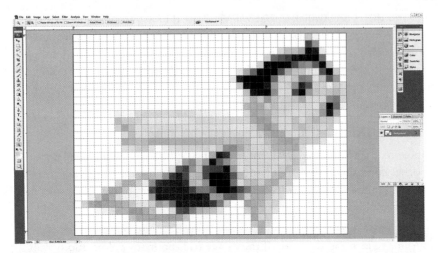

FIGURE 5.35   Reduce the image size and lay gridlines over the image.

FIGURE 5.36   The image copied line by line into *Minecraft*.

Sculpting a 3D Statue

Creating a statue for your world can be extremely challenging, but is entirely worthwhile. There are a few methods to accomplish this, and we'll have a look at them now.

The most manually intensive way involves the patient artistry of chipping away at a megalith, block by block, until you reveal your inner masterpiece. It's best to have a well-thought-out concept plan to guide you beforehand and then channel your inner Michelangelo to completion!

The second way involves an extension of your 2D pixel art to include the depth of the image as well. Some brilliant freeware solutions are available that will convert any 3D image into a schematic that you can use for your build. As with creating 2D pixel art, you'll need to have image-editing software installed.

If you're looking for an existing 3D model to hone your skills on, try visiting a site such as Qblock (http://kyucon.com/qblock), where users have built schematics for a wide variety of objects, shapes, and anime characters for online sharing. You can edit colors and block placement and spin the model 360 degrees. View each separate layer in the schematic, page by page, and follow the pattern onscreen to replicate it with colored blocks in your *Minecraft* world, as I have demonstrated in Figure 5.37.

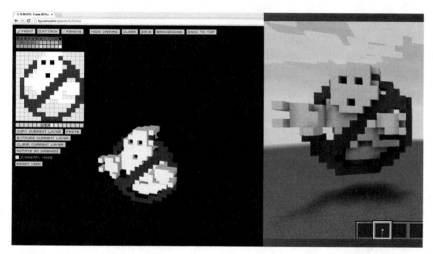

FIGURE 5.37 Re-create your statue, layer by layer, using schematics created yourself from a 3D conversion program or using a freeware solution such as the *Ghostbusters* no-ghost sign from Qblock.

To create your own 3D model, you'll need to access a content-creation program such as Blender (http://blender.org) or Trimble SketchUp (www.sketchup.com). These are free, open-source programs; however, there are many others available.

If you have an existing 3D model that you wish to convert to pixelated form (called voxelization), conversion programs such as Binvox are available (http://www.patrickmin. com/minecraft). Once your file is in a *Minecraft*-compatible format (.schematic), you can import it into *Minecraft* using an open-source world editor such as MCEdit (see Figure 5.38).

FIGURE 5.38   Add mobs and resources to your world using MCEdit.

MCEdit allows you to alter the physical attributes of your *Minecraft* world by adding 3D shapes, changing the components of your landscape and the size of individual attributes, flattening, deleting, or expanding sections, and even changing the appearance and placement of mobs and other resources. In this example, we are downloading a large house build into our existing world (see Figures 5.39 and 5.40). An extensive collection of builds is available for download at Minecraft-Schematics.com, such as this Steampunk House created by user Mad_Mr_Potato.

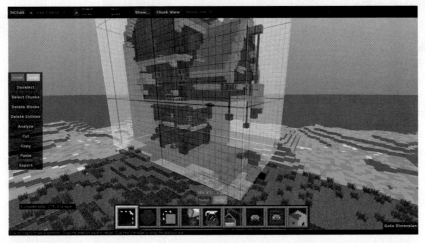

FIGURE 5.39   Importing a .schematic file into your *Minecraft* world using MCEdit gives you the ability to add large structures in minutes.

FIGURE 5.40   Once you have imported your own .schematic 3D file, the object will appear in the same position in your *Minecraft* world, ready for use.

Creating Spheres, Circles, and Arches

Some brilliant, free online conversion programs are available to plot your circle or sphere. Simply enter your block radius to generate a pattern that you can build into your *Minecraft* world. Have a look at these great sites to get started: www.mineconics.net and **www. plotz.co.uk**. The Filler Machine in Buildcraft can also achieve this in-game (see Chapter 7, "Empire Building with BuildCraft").

If you are looking to build an exceptionally large circular structure, dome, or sphere and want to save (a lot) of time, you could, of course, jump into a mod to alter your world behind the scenes. Try using the time-saving filter at http://sethbling.com/createrotatedsolid to build your monolith, using a single slice as the cross-section of your anticipated whole. The slice will rotate 360 degrees around its center point to build a solid object. Remember to back up your existing build first, and make sure you create the object in a space far clear of other structures to prevent an override.

If you prefer the Michelangelo approach (blood, sweat, and tears), you can create an impressive build armed with only your pickaxe and plunder. In the following example, I've used different colored rings, corresponding to the circular pattern in Figure 5.41 to demonstrate the manual creation of a spherical home in the sky (see Figure 4.43):

1. Create a vertical circle following the pattern that best suits the size of the sphere you need. Each quarter segment must be identical.

2. If you're planning a floating sphere, pillar jump high enough to begin and then knock it away.

3. Create a second circle intersecting at the center-top and -bottom blocks of the original circle.

FIGURE 5.41   Keep each quarter pattern identical.

4. Follow your blocks out in a radial pattern until each forms a complete ring, as per Figure 5.42. Add an additional block in arm's length as you progress closer to the center, which should be the widest point on your circle.

FIGURE 5.42   As you progress, check that your rings are symmetrical.

5. Once your rings are in place, fill in the gaps from the inside—you don't want to change the exterior shape of your rings.

FIGURE 5.43   A floating retreat—time to begin interior design.

Building in the Nether and End Regions

Construction Elements: Build a high fortress using cobblestone or Netherbrick—make sure your mining tunnels are covered by glass. A tree farm (BYO dirt) will provide resources for tools, torches, charcoal, and building.

Complementary Building Materials: Magma cubes, Netherbrick, end stone, Nether quartz, obsidian, gravel, and Netherrack.

Complementary Decorations: Ender crystals, obsidian, dragon eggs, glowstone, and soul sand.

As unappealing as the Nether can be, you can build impressive farms, forests, and homes in the underworld and alter your environment significantly—but plan ahead to make sure you don't waste precious resources.

Cobblestone and glass are your main building materials in the Nether. Before you head underground, mine a large quantity of sand to smelt to glass in your furnace. In the Nether, cobblestone has similar properties to obsidian, which makes it a durable resource for building. It's relatively easy to find in the Overworld, so chances are, you've got a fair bit stashed in your inventory already.

In the Nether, take advantage of the height of natural formations of Netherrack to give you an eagle's-eye view of the landscape. Begin by building a high, enclosed safety room with 360-degree glass windows—no nasty surprises. A strong defensive base is especially important if you're tackling a multiplayer server game.

Try climbing up wall ladders and throwing an Ender Pearl into the bedrock (or placing a hatch) to use as a base. It's a great place to stash your chests in PvP mode—but take enough materials to build back down so it's not a one-way trip! Also keep in mind that if you build a Nether Portal in the bedrock to escape back into the Overworld, it won't serve as an entry into the Nether at your original position, so take your map so you can find your way back home in the Overworld.

Connect your living areas, mining tunnels, and observation decks with glass to protect yourself from the ghast. You don't want your hard work blown apart.

Hide multiple entrances to your Nether base in case you need a quick escape to safety. Make sure they have doors (and perhaps a hidden lever) to keep the nasties out.

If you're after a more natural habitat, smelt Netherrack to create Netherbrick and then repair and fortify an abandoned Nether Fortress by crafting walls, stairs, slabs, and fences.

Build a tree farm so you don't have to keep returning to the Overworld to harvest wood. Don't attempt to fast-grow a tree unless you're sure you have enough space; otherwise, your bone meal will be wasted. Of course, empty growing space means ghasts, too, so place glowstone and glass within your tree farm in an efficient pattern to prevent spawning, as well as providing your saplings with necessary light. If you're crop farming, in the absence of water, tilled land must be planted immediately to prevent it reverting to dirt. Plants will grow slightly slower than normal in the Nether.

If you're planning on extensive mining or multiple bases, bring an empty map and activate it in the Nether. You can build a rail system to cover your entire map using fewer resources due to the 3:1 size ratio. Place redstone under one in every 15 bricks as your power source.

If building in the End is more your style, or you're planning an Enderman farm to harvest Ender Pearls, a semi-permanent residence to house your portal can be an advantage. Keep your house mob proof by creating a moat around it so Endermen can't teleport in. You'll need to bring in any building materials from the Overworld (or Nether Fortress) because there is nothing to mine in the End but the yellow-green abyss of End Stone and the odd obsidian column.

The Bottom Line

The best way to improve your build is, of course, to build. The more you expand on your existing ideas and try new techniques, the more quickly your expertise will develop. There are brilliant software programs now available that give you unprecedented control over your landscape and modeling, so take advantage of the wealth of creative license you have access to.

Construction can take time, but the satisfaction of seeing your creation come to pixelated life is well worth the effort. Whatever you do, don't give up on your ideas! If you get stuck, simply search for inspiration from your community of fellow Minecraft architects and get back to it—remember, *Minecraft* Rome wasn't built in a day (apparently it took five months!). You can download the entire project from http://www.planetminecraft.com/project/roman-city-download/ (http://goo.gl/E8Nqdn).

More Power to You

In This Chapter

- Learn to create smarter dimmer switches.
- Craft a new combo for your castle.
- Build a minecart stopover system.
- See red with one of *Minecraft*'s best mods.
- Forget redstone—get wired.

Remember all those lengthy runs of repeaters, bulky AND gates, and other circuits from the previous chapters? What if you could reduce them down to just a few clever components? How about building a fancy combination lock for your door? Or what about creating an automated switching system that can send a minecart quietly running around every automated farm picking up all the goods and bringing them home. Also, what if the farms just did all that growing and harvesting on their own without you needing to push a single button? You'll find all that and more in this exploration of more advanced redstone circuits and a mod that adds a multitude of possibilities to the construction of more powerful devices.

Combination Lock

There are times—you'll undoubtedly encounter them—when the standard redstone system can seem maddeningly complicated. A case in point: The addition of rotatable items within frames. The ability to read their position through a comparator, opens up some possibilities:

- Item frames become rheostats, able to output a varying voltage. The closest you may have seen this in the real world is the humble dimmer switch. We'll build one for the house. Mood lighting—ahhh, perfect for that quiet dinner in front of the fire. (A note for Spinal Tap fans: The frame is limited to eight positions, so you won't be able to crank it up to 11.)
- Although combination locks have been done many times before, the additions to *Minecraft* v1.8 allow them to be done in a very different way: Instead of pushing buttons in a particular order, one can now rotate the items in a frame, like the tumblers on a bike chain lock. There are eight

possible settings for each dial, so just a set of three will deliver 8×8×8 (or 512) potential combinations.

So where's the complication? Creating dimmer switches is easy. I'll show you how in just a few steps. But combo locks? The problem comes in setting the lock. It would be very nice to be able to dial in a combination, push a button, and set those values, but *Minecraft* lacks an easy way to store a current value. The creation of such a device would involve building something like an analog-to-digital converter, and such projects, although possible, quickly spiral into spaghetti-like complexity. But there is a good solution, and you'll learn how. First, though, let's take a look at rotatable item frames because they're an interesting addition. Follow these steps (Figure 6.1 shows the end result):

1. Place down any opaque block, such as wood, and attach an item frame to the front.

2. Insert your favorite item into the frame. I'm using a severed creeper's head, although I wasn't personally responsible.

3. Place a comparator against the back of the block, leading out behind, and run a redstone trail for eight blocks.

4. Place a line of redstone lamps next to the trail.

5. Now head back to the item frame and right-click it. You'll see the inserted item rotate through eight possible positions with the lamps lighting up in sequence.

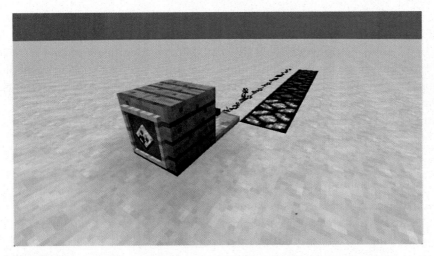

FIGURE 6.1 A line of lamps controlled from the item frame.

You can build dimmers wherever, of course, but if the actual dimmer is some distance from the first light, use a string of comparators to deliver the current to the first lamp. This will keep the power setting until it reaches the right location. Using a repeater to boost the current will spoil its ability to dim correctly.

Anyway, let's head back to combo locks.

There are two alternatives for combination locks: One is to use hidden item frames to set the code and then use a circuit to compare their values against those being dialed in at the doorway. The other is to build a lock where the combination is already dialed in due to a line of physical blocks.

The first method takes a little bit of work because the redstone comparator, while in *compare* mode, only serves to show if a signal is equal to or greater than another. Therefore, it needs another comparison to also find out if the signal is equal to or less than another. It then will only enact when both are positive at the same time, which means the values are equal.

But it's not really work if you're having fun, and this happens to be a great way to learn a couple of useful redstone concepts. (I'll show you the other version next.) Just follow these steps:

1. Start by laying the base components shown in Figure 6.2. There are four comparators and, in the bottom right, a repeater facing toward the wall. Don't forget to place two drops of redstone dust and the redstone torch shown on top of the block.

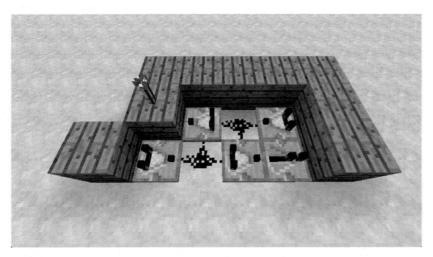

FIGURE 6.2 Creating the base platform.

2. Figure 6.3 shows a view from the back. Place the item frame against the face of the middle block (this frame will be used to set the combination), and then any item you like inside, and a redstone torch on the left. You'll also need two other blocks on top of the sidewall to prevent different strands of redstone from getting mixed up. You could also use two redstone repeaters facing toward the back wall shown in the figure.

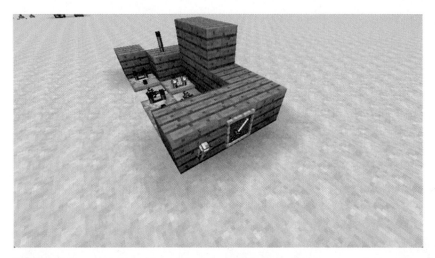

FIGURE 6.3 Place any item you like inside the frame.

3. Run a trail of redstone from the upright torch, over the block wall, and down to the ground, as shown in Figure 6.4, so that it meets the torch placed against the back wall. Okay, almost done.

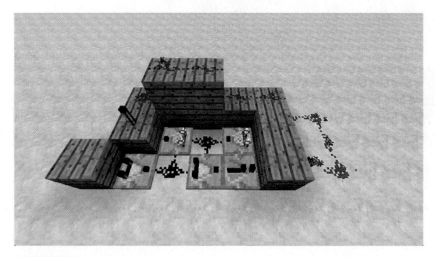

FIGURE 6.4 Connecting the dots (or torches) with redstone.

4. Place another item frame against the very front block shown in Figure 6.5.

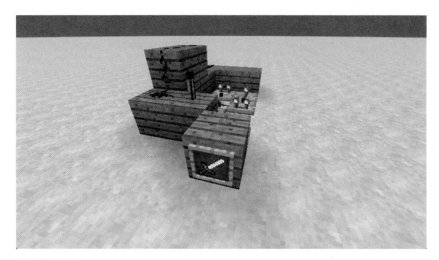

FIGURE 6.5 This item frame provides the input that is compared to the setting of the other.

5. Finally, place the block, torch, and lamp shown in Figure 6.6, and run the redstone over the top of the block.

FIGURE 6.6 The final piece of the combination puzzle.

How does this work? Take a look at Figure 6.7. The comparators leading away from each item frame don't do any comparing or any other type of logical calculation. They simply feed out a signal equal to the rotation angle of the item in the frame, from 1 to 8. It's the two comparators in the middle that do all the work.

FIGURE 6.7 Testing the system.

I'm about to get into some Boolean logic, so feel free to skip the next four paragraphs if this will bore you to tears. However, if you care to bear with me, and you're not quite sure how comparators work, here's what's going on: In compare mode (a comparator's default setting), a signal comes in from behind and is passed on if it equals or is greater than the signal coming in from the side. Therefore, the leftmost comparator on the bottom row (just before the repeater) gets its main signal from the back as well as the side signal from the redstone linked to the comparator on its top right. If the item frame on the left (what will become the front) is equal or higher, a positive signal goes to the repeater, then through the block to turn off the redstone torch.

Meanwhile, the comparator in the right-hand position of the top row receives the signal from the code-setting item frame at the back, compares it to the one from the front item frame, and only sends its signal if its item frame has an equal or higher setting.

In a logical sense, if one circuit can light only if it is equal to or greater than the other, and the other can only light up if it is equal to or less than the other, then the satisfaction to this quandary is that they can only light up if they are equal.

So, now we have two circuits that provide an output if they are true, but in reality both outputs are passed through inverters by virtue of the redstone torches, meaning that only if they are both off will the final torch beside the redstone lamp light up.

The logical goal (for reasons relating to eventually doing something useful with the signals that doesn't require a plethora of AND gates) is to provide a signal on either line only if the item frame values don't match, and then invert that just before it reaches the redstone lamp so that the lamp lights up only if they do match. This saves a lot of additional wiring and is the equivalent of a NOR gate.

This is a modular design, so you can easily repeat it, for example, to set up a series of code tumblers, such as is shown in Figure 6.8, and then build an entry around it running the redstone output from the back to lock everything off, as shown in Figures 6.9 and 6.10.

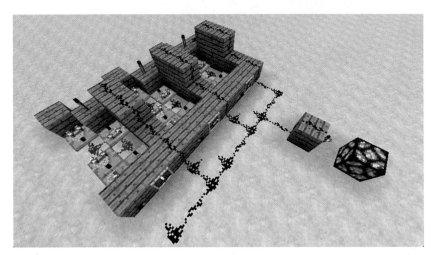

FIGURE 6.8 Creating a series of tumblers, linking their output.

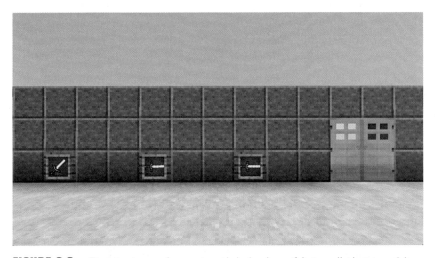

FIGURE 6.9 Front view of a potential design. Note all the tumblers can be placed one block higher, if you prefer, just by lifting all the blocks up one level.

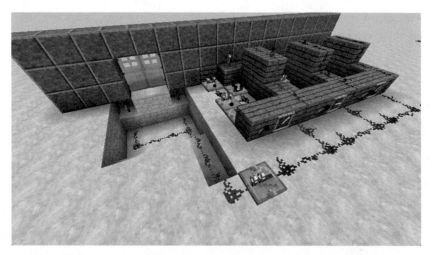

FIGURE 6.10   And the rear view of the same setup.

Repeat the layout as many times as you like. Because each lock has eight possible settings, adding a second frame set will provide 64 combinations, while a third will increase this to 512.

If this seems a little convoluted, you may want to consider a different design. It's worth mentioning simply to show how thinking outside the box can deliver quick results. This is based on a demonstration provided by *Minecraft* legend SethBling, and is elegant in its design, although it relies on setting the length of a string of blocks to create the input code.

Take a look at Figure 6.11. The leftmost block has the item frame on its face, although you can't see it in the figure. Moving from left to right, the next block is the comparator to deliver the signal from the frame. The alternating colored blocks in the middle set the code for the frame. In this case, I've set it to the third position through the virtue of those three blocks, but you can use anything from one to eight blocks.

The last of the code blocks has a redstone torch placed on its side, and the final block in the row is needed to reduce the power count by one before it gets boosted by the repeater. This is because item frames output power from one to eight, but we need to subtract one here so a power output of three from the comparator reaches zero before the repeater.

Here's what happens: If the power output is less than three, the redstone torch lights up, feeding the redstone running below. If the power is greater than three, the signal prevents the torch from lighting but stretches the four blocks until it reaches the repeater, lighting up the redstone trail anyway. Only if it is exactly three does the trail not light up.

This layout is highly modular and can be made with one less gap between each of the code inputs than the previous example. In fact, wiring is easy, too: Just ensure no wires cross-link before the repeaters at the end of each row. It doesn't matter what happens after that, so you can dig tunnels under the rows to link the wires up at the torch end, or whatever fits. Remember, though, that as in the other example, the signal is inverted, so you flip it with a redstone torch placed under the door, or invert it somewhere beforehand if you'll use the current to directly power the doors. Figure 6.12 shows a block of three tumblers set to positions three, six, and four.

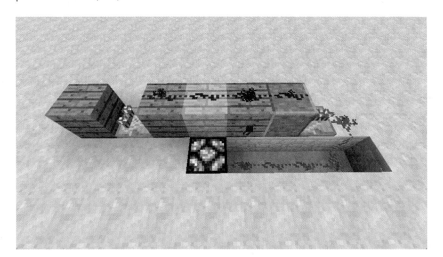

FIGURE 6.11 Using a string of blocks to create the combination setting.

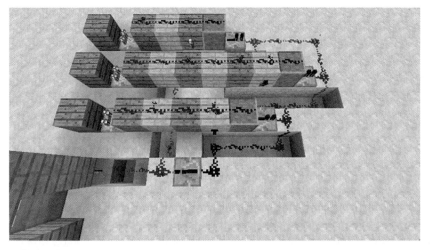

FIGURE 6.12 String the rows together with redstone, in whatever way works to complete this design.

TIP

Protecting Blocks from Damage

In vanilla *Minecraft* it might seem like there's not much point in using combination locks. Any player can break through a wall with a pickaxe. However, most *Minecraft* servers implement a system called WorldGuard that does permit an area to be assigned to a player or group of players that will allow only them to break and place blocks. If you want to do this in a single player, LAN-shared game, or a basic server, use something such as the Permissions Mod—there are quite a few that do the same thing—to specify a protected area that will prevent other players from breaking through, placing TNT, and general griefing. It currently works with v1.6.4 and can be downloaded from http://goo.gl/Afw6C9.

So, there you have two combo lock designs. Remember to close the door as you leave...just change those front tumblers.

Minecart Switches

In Chapter 2, "Automated Produce Farms," you saw how to create farms with minecart-based collection points that allow for the loading and unloading of minecarts, as well as an automated sorter.

In this section I want to show you how to tie everything together so that a single minecart can travel to every farm, pick up the produce, and bring it all back to base. This helps prevent dealing with collisions between minecarts as they head back to the sorter (I don't think they have properly licensed drivers) and saves running loads of additional minecart tracks. What's more, you can tie the harvesting of every farm to a single button push. In other words, stand at the sorter, push one button, all the harvesting will start automatically, and the minecart will push off, visiting each farm in turn to collect the results, and return to the sorter where everything can be unloaded automatically. Sounds pretty neat, and you already have nearly all the pieces in place.

The first part of the system is also the key—using detector rails to change the setting of a T-intersection in a minecart track. You can see how it works in Figure 6.13.

Any tracks meeting at a T-intersection gain a switching capability at the top of the track that is in the middle of the intersection—the curved one you can see in the image. Adding any power source to the track makes it switch. One of the more convenient ways to do this is by sticking a lever in the ground, as you can see in the image; however, you can do other things such as placing a daylight sensor in the same position to set up automatic routing. This is especially useful if you are riding the cart and wish to automatically zoom off home as darkness falls, taking a shortcut, so to speak.

FIGURE 6.13 String the rows together with redstone, in whatever way works to complete this design.

But this doesn't help an unattended minecart get around the track. Detector rails provide the solution. If you look at Figure 6.14, you'll see an easy to follow pattern. Place the detector rails at least two track sections back from the meeting point of the junction and run the redstone out two blocks as well so that it also has the chance to run into the tip of the junction; otherwise, it won't trigger.

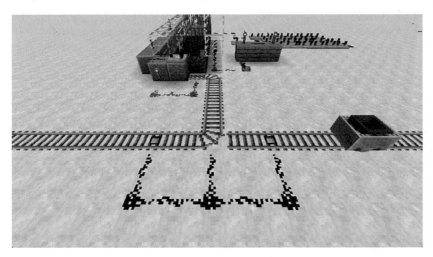

FIGURE 6.14 Follow this pattern to alternate the track between destinations.

You'll notice as you create these junctions that they'll always bend to the east when unpowered and to the west when powered. This may lead to some interesting routing while the cart travels, but it will always end up back at the start.

There's just one last thing to be done—connect everything up to the sorter. You can do that by using the automatic minecart unloading system from Chapter 2. Figure 6.15 shows an example.

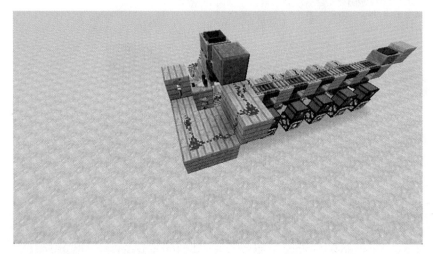

FIGURE 6.15   Adding the automatic unloader to the sorter. Make sure you have powered rails in place to get the minecart up the ramp!

Project:Red

Now we get to the good stuff—and I don't necessarily mean Bono's project Red. This Project:Red is a mod that adds an incredible amount of functionality to *Minecraft*'s redstone system. It solves all the difficult problems by adding new logic gates that reduce what are huge constructions down to a single very powerful chip. Its wires can run up walls and even around corners; they can be bundled together, then unbundled, so you can run multiple redstone signals at once through a single strand and then separate them at the end. Oh, and the redstone current can run for over 250 blocks, as compared to the usual 15. It also adds new types of sensors, and includes Forge Multipart (see the following note). You'll also find new world-generation features such as the addition of volcanoes, new types of blocks and trees, very cool-looking lanterns, and more. However, we're going to focus on the electronics and wiring side.

The current release of this mod is designed for v1.6.4 of *Minecraft*, and there are quite a few required files. However, it's easy enough to install if you use a mod loader such as MultiMC, introduced in Chapter 1, "Getting Started."

NOTE

What Is Forge Multipart?

Multipart is a change to the block system in *Minecraft* that allows multiple blocks of different types to fit into a single space. All it takes is a saw, which you'll find as a new item in the inventory. Then you take almost any other block in the game and combine it with the saw to create smaller blocks. You can change the resultant block type by adjusting the crafting recipe, and you can then take those smaller blocks and shave them down once more. The size goes down quite a few levels. But perhaps even better is that this change to block space management allows other items to fit into a single space. For example, levers, buttons, redstone torches, and so on can all be placed inside a single block space, against the walls of other blocks, solving what often becomes a difficult problem in designing active systems. If you want to learn more, watch the following video by direwolf20: http://goo.gl/iDlbJw.

If you want to install this mod on its own, without it being part of a mod pack, you'll find the downloads at http://projectredwiki.com/wiki/Version_archive. Check to ensure it's still v1.7.2 because the mods are often updated; then visit http://files.minecraftforge.net/CodeChickenLib/ and select the corresponding *Universal* version of that mod. (You may need to select the option **View Legacy Builds** to find the correct version.) Install both into the same instance of *Minecraft* created in MultiMC, as described in Chapter 1, ensuring Forge is also installed, and you'll be ready to go.

TIP

Too Many Items?

The number of items added by Project:Red is astounding, and their crafting recipes are often very complex. I'm going to focus on Creative mode here so we don't need to list all the recipes. Really, it will take too long to go through it all. However, you can also use this mod in Survival mode, hence the addition of the new trees, blocks, and so on to the generated world that provide the necessary crafting ingredients. If you want to give that a try, download a mod called "Not Enough Items" (actually a re-creation of an out-of-date mod called "Too Many Items"—hence this tip's title). Now, when you open your inventory you'll see all the available items on the right of the screen. Hover your mouse over any item and press **R** to view its recipe or **U** to see all the recipes in which it is used. You won't be able to take any of the items, but seeing their recipes and uses is invaluable. NEI, as it is usually called, has a multitude of further options available, including being able to set up to seven save points (see Figure 6.16). Although not quite nine lives, you'll appreciate every one of them. You can see them all by starting a world in Creative mode or by ensuring cheats are enabled in a Survival world and then typing **/gamemode creative**, taking a sneak peek, and then heading back to Survival by typing, you guessed it, **/gamemode survival**. You'll find NEI at http://goo.gl/IBeYCl—it's well worth getting to know.

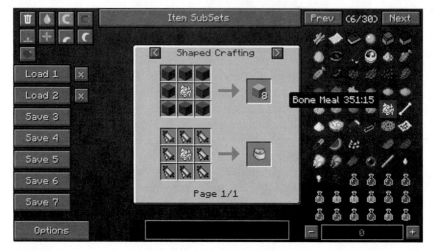

FIGURE 6.16   Not Enough Items mod showing the uses for bone meal.

Automating a Pumpkin Farm

To get started with Project:Red, let's return to one of the examples from Chapter 2, with all of that crazy wiring, repeaters, and logic gates built from blocks and torches and wiring (see Figure 6.17 as a reminder). In this example, we had an AND gate that would only allow the water to be sent cascading down the pumpkin patch if the pistons had been raised. With Project:Red, there are easier ways to do this. In fact, it will only take four main components, some wiring, and a trusty screwdriver to create not only the farm from Chapter 2, but one that looks after its own growth and harvesting. Add that to the automatic collection and sorting system, and it's a completely hands-off experience.

FIGURE 6.17   Yes, we're all back on the pumpkin patch.

You'll need the following items from the inventory:

- **Red alloy wiring**—This is vastly superior to redstone because it not only has a 255-block transmission distance but, as mentioned earlier, can run up walls, around corners, and even along ceilings. It also can't be washed away by water, which is true of all the Project:Red components. (This is always a dire danger when using the standard redstone resources and working with water. It's like the Creeper meme "I just undid in 5 seconds what you spent the last 5 hours building.") You'll find the wiring under the Project:Red Transmission tab in Page 2 of the inventory.

- **Repeater**—The Project:Red repeater works the same way as the standard redstone version, with the advantage of being able to set a higher delay. However, we're just using it as a diode to prevent current from flowing in the wrong direction. It's under the Integration tab, as are the next three items.

- **State cell**—This is a very handy device that can keep current flowing for as long as required after receiving a single pulse. It can also be locked with another current, and that's the key to making the farm failsafe.

- **Pulse former**—This component converts a sustained current into a single pulse, which is exactly what's required to keep the dispenser under control.

- **Sequencer**—This is the master controller, providing the main loop required to allow the crops to grow.

- **Screwdriver**—This is an essential tool because a right-click with the screwdriver allows the orientation of any of the components to be adjusted. A Shift-right-click is also used for configuring some of the more advanced components in useful ways. It's under the Core tab.

- ***Minecraft* components**—And last but not least, the design also uses a standard lever from the redstone section of the inventory, as well as the sticky piston and a dispenser filled with a bucket of Evian (but if you can't find that, standard H2O will do).

Figure 6.18 shows a schematic of the layout.

So, how does this work? The challenge is to ensure that the water that harvests the crop never has the chance to flow down and wash away the pumpkin (or melon) stems, so this means the pistons need to be up and stay up until any water from the dispenser has finished harvesting the crop and has also completely dried up.

Everything begins with the sequencer (2). It can be placed in any direction, and a right-click with the mouse (not the screwdriver) will allow you to set the interval between harvests. Pumpkins can pop up quite rapidly, so an interval of 300 to 600 seconds, depending on how full you'd like the row in the farm, will work well. By the way, the only bad news I have here is that if you did build the farm from Chapter 2 already, there's no way to import it back into this version of *Minecraft*, so it will need to be started over.

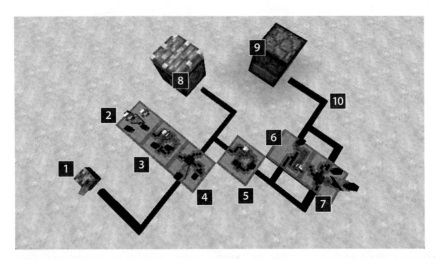

FIGURE 6.18 Components that automate the harvest. The process flows from left to right.

1 Standard lever

2 Sequencer: the harvest growth time

3 Pulse former

4 State cell: the harvesting period

5 Pulse former

6 Repeater

7 State cell

8 Sticky piston

9 Dispenser: the water flow control

10 Red alloy wiring

The sequencer's only job is to provide the first pulse to set everything else in motion, so it could actually be replaced with a standard block and a redstone button, but then it wouldn't be fully *fully* automatic.

Sequencers provide a sustained current while they're passing through any of the cardinal points, and that's where the pulse former (3) bursts into action. Pulse formers convert sustained current into a 2-tick pulse, or 1/10th of a second of real time.

The state cell (4) converts that pulse into something that can be tuned to suit the requirement of the pistons being up in the air while the harvest takes place. When placed, the rotating head on top will point to the left. It looks an awful lot like an arrow and will seem to be facing the wrong way rather than directly ahead, but it's okay. See Figure 6.19 for a close-up.

The water needs to flow for about 8 seconds. Because the current from this one raises the pistons beforehand, and the pistons need to outlast the water by a reasonable safety margin, right-click it to set a time of 16 seconds.

State cells are useful because any current exiting from the left remains sustained for the entire set clock time. Anything exiting the front just receives a pulse at the end of the set time, and anything entering from the right resets the clock but is still passed through, which is perfect for locking down the entire system.

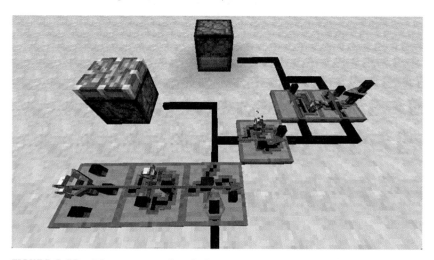

FIGURE 6.19 The arrows lead the way, and a right-click with the screwdriver can rotate any if they land askew.

The next pulse former (5) converts the sustained current from the state cell into another quick burst so that the signals to the dispenser can be handled with care. That burst hits the repeater (6) and follows the trail straight to the dispenser, turning on the water supply. It also hits the second state cell (7), kicking off its timing cycle. Once complete, the current exits from the front of the cell as a new pulse, hits the dispenser, and pulls back in the water block placed with the first, thus cutting off the flow. Set this one for 8 seconds. The repeater (6) is facing toward the dispenser, and because repeaters only allow current to flow in one direction, it prevents the pulse from sauntering back into the circuit that feeds the state cell (7). Without that repeater, this would cause an endless loop of pulses continuously hitting the dispenser.

The best way really to understand this is to replicate the design and see it in action. Lay the red alloy wiring (10) as shown, and dig a little three-block-long trench in front of the dispenser to prevent a flood. Set the sequencer to something smaller such as 60 seconds so you're not waiting 10 minutes to see the first hit!

Figure 6.20 shows the entire system hooked up to the original pumpkin farm.

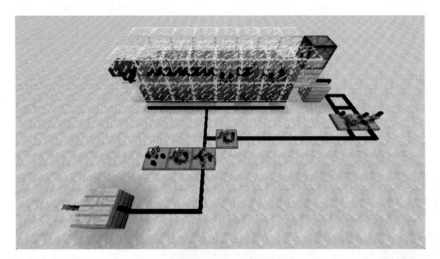

FIGURE 6.20 A fully automated pumpkin farm. Finally, something useful, eh?

What Else Can Project:Red Do?

So glad you asked. Actually, it's an incredibly formidable mod. Up to now it's still only a partial rewrite of Red Power 2—probably one of the most respected mods that has ever existed but has since fallen into disrepair—but new features are being added fast.

As you may have surmised from the number of install files and additions to the inventory menus, Project:Red can do a whole lot more. It's divided into four major components.

Core

Core contains support systems for the rest of the mod, including all the objects used in crafting and interacting with other objects.

Integration

This category contains all the logic gates—those components such as the sequencer, state cell, and so on. But it goes far, far beyond. Although these components include those such as the state cell and many others, such as counters, that are either ferociously difficult to accomplish in standard *Minecraft* or just plain impossible, there are some that are easily understandable. And, by the way, I won't go through them all because they are numerous, but here are a few to whet your appetite, with their *Minecraft* counterparts:

- **AND gate**—The AND gate provides up to three inputs—if all are positive, it will provide an output (see Figure 6.21). However, it can also be configured to use just one (which is not really helpful) with a Shift-right-click of the screwdriver. But like all the Project:Red components, it can also be placed against any block face, which is brilliant for tight circuits. In addition, using insulated cables (more on that later) ensures the wires don't cross-join.

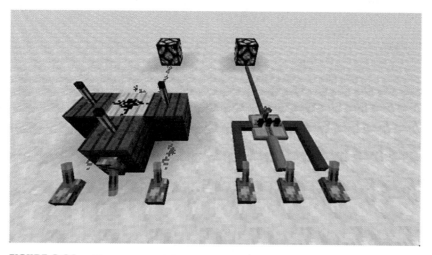

FIGURE 6.21   Three-way *Minecraft* AND gate on the left, and the Project:Red version on the right.

- **XOR gate**—These gates, shown in Figure 6.22, can be used in all sorts of ways. The output turns on only if one input is on and the other is off, but it doesn't matter which ones are doing the on and off. They're like those switches that turn a central light on in the middle of the room, or off, from either end. In fact, you could use it to do just that: Turn on a series of redstone lamps at the front door, turn them off at the other, and so on. There are all kinds of uses. Use it as a circuit that can lift a drawbridge out of the water at one end and let it down at the other, or use it as a circuit to open a hidden doorway, then walk through and close it on the other side.

- **Randomizer**—Okay, I'm having fun with this one. The only way I can imagine creating a randomizer in *Minecraft* is by trapping some poor pig in a cage where he then wanders between pressure plates. The randomizer makes it so much easier (see Figure 6.23).

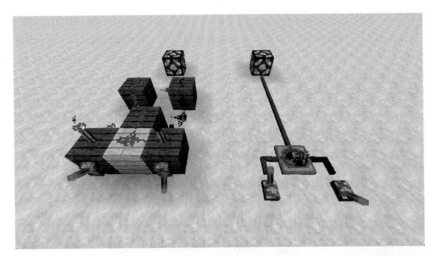

FIGURE 6.22 Three-way *Minecraft* XOR gate on the left, and the Project:Red version on the right.

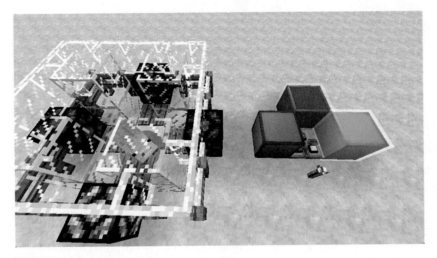

FIGURE 6.23 Disco lights, anyone?

Transmission

This is the wiring category, and it might change how you try to do anything using redstone power in *Minecraft*. Many capabilities can be combined in various impressive ways, but I'll give just two examples here:

■ **Climbing and bending**—Wires can climb walls, run along ceilings, be hidden by covers, and generally just free you up to wire a house or solve any other problems with consummate ease (see Figure 6.24).

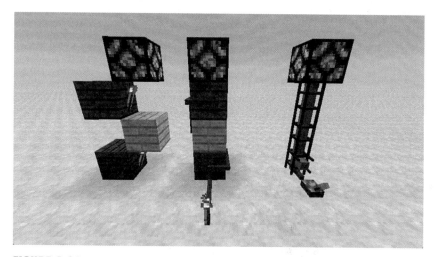

FIGURE 6.24 The usual way of ascending power on the left, a piece of red alloy wiring from Project:Red in the middle, showing off as it snakes its way around the column, and another method to build a tower using framed wire on the right.

■ **Bundling**—Bundling allows up to 16 insulated wires to run together through a single cable with their different power states separating out correctly at the other side (see Figure 6.25).

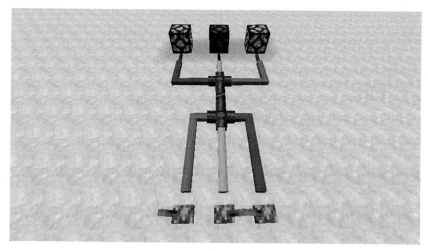

FIGURE 6.25 Confound those currents with bundling. Try doing that with redstone.

Transportation

This is not about motoring around. This type of transportation refers to the moving of items from one storage container to another through a network of pipes. Think of it like a far more sophisticated version of the automated sorting system from Chapter 2. The storage minecart that has been running around picking up everything from the automated farms unloads its goods into a chest that is connected to the pipe network. Each other chest can request from that main storage the items it should specifically store. At the same time a hopper attached to a furnace could request items to smelt that are coming up from a mine, and those completed items could be sent to another chest. Finally, a crafting pipe attached to the network can request the ingredients to turn them into various completed items.

Figure 6.26 provides a very simplified view of the capabilities, but this is something we'll be looking at in the next chapter with another astonishing mod.

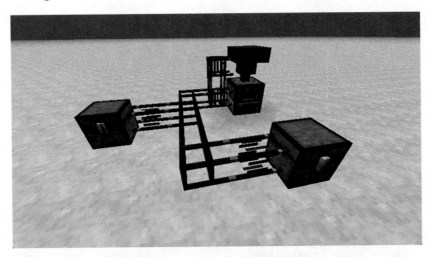

FIGURE 6.26   A simple transportation pipe network. There is more in store.

The Bottom Line

Redstone itself is remarkable in its inherent capabilities, but can seem something like a Bach fugue: Once one digs deeper, the complexity proves never ending.

What begins as an understanding of what really is a quite limited smattering of core components can become a constant exploration in discovering different ways of making them work together to achieve a particular result.

A lot of tutorials online cover redstone, and there is an entire chapter in *The Ultimate Player's Guide to Minecraft, Second Edition* devoted to core redstone concepts that covers all its components with many examples. However, it can prove frustrating to achieve even simple things. (Search online for examples of three-way minecart switching stations, for example.) Mods such as Project:Red make so many things so much easier. Just the ability to run wires together without them intersecting into a frustrating mass of redstone brings a joy to the design of automated systems—and I didn't even mention the beautiful lanterns and other lights built in. To learn more, see the mod's home page at http://projectredwiki.com.

It doesn't take long to put this mod's components together into simple systems that do wonderful things. However, stand by as the next chapter introduces another fabulous mod: BuildCraft.

Empire Building with BuildCraft

In This Chapter

- Create an automated sorter with pipes.
- Use engines to create a power system.
- Dig huge automated quarries to gather numerous resources.
- Use pumps to shift liquid assets.
- Refine oil into fuel to produce even more power.
- Save and re-create structures using blueprints automatically.

BuildCraft adds numerous features to *Minecraft*. You can use it to create automated mining machines, transport fluids and blocks through pipes, control the pipes and associated engines with logic blocks that respond to a variety of events, and then perform a specific action. It vastly simplifies item sorting, can store structures as blueprints and replicate on demand, automatically craft items, and a whole lot more.

BuildCraft Core Concepts

The BuildCraft mod is available from http://www.mod-buildcraft.com/download/ (http://goo.gl/26jvFU). It requires Forge, and both are installed in the usual way (see Chapter 1, "Getting Started"), and at this writing has been updated to work with *Minecraft* v1.7.10.

As with all well-designed mods, you can craft from scratch every item in BuildCraft when playing on Survival. The items also appear under additional tabs in the Creative inventory and work perfectly well with the Not Enough Items (NEI) mod so you can easily discover each item's crafting recipe, although you can also find those and more information on the BuildCraft Wiki at http://goo.gl/WEFz4S.

BuildCraft is composed of several key sections, a few of which are shown in Figure 7.1:

- **Block and Fluid Transport**—Like in Project:Red (see Chapter 6, "More Power to You"), *transport* refers to moving objects between various inventories, tanks, and machines using pipes. See the section "Pipe Dreams" for more on this.

- **Engines and Energy**—BuildCraft uses engines to power pipes, factories, and other objects. There are three types of engine with varying fuel and cooling requirements, and different levels of energy output. Managing the energy produced from the two more powerful is an important part of the design of any automation system because failing to do so can result in a catastrophic explosion. Fortunately, energy management can be automated using BuildCraft's logic gates.

- **Factories**—Think of factories as automated objects. They include crafting machines and mineral extraction via powered quarries and mining wells.

- **Oil and Fluid Extraction**—BuildCraft includes pumps that can extract lava, water, and oil from the landscape. You wouldn't have seen oil previously. It's a new type of fluid added to worlds that are generated with BuildCraft installed. The oil appears as pools on the ground and in the ocean, and also as oil springs that spurt high into the air.

- **Automated Construction**—Copy any set of blocks and convert them into a blueprint that can be reused over and over, and even shared with other players on the same server, sent via email, and so on. The mod also includes a builder system that can create 3D primitives such as pyramids, cylinders, hollow cubes, and other structures, or quickly flatten areas so you don't need to remove blocks by hand.

FIGURE 7.1 An automated BuildCraft quarry with engines and a sorting system.

In addition, BuildCraft is undergoing constant development. Although not available at this writing, the next release (v6.1) will add a variety of robots that can fight mobs, harvest produce, passive mobs, and trees, and also plant farms.

There's a lot in this mod: It's one of the most complete mods available for *Minecraft*. Let's start with some basic concepts and turn them into working machines.

Pipe Dreams

Much of BuildCraft is based on the idea of moving items, fluids, or energy through pipes, and then doing something useful with those resources at the other end.

Remember the rather complicated item sorting system from Chapter 6? Let's take a look at how incredibly easy it is to replicate this functionality in BuildCraft. As with many of the other chapters, I recommend you try this in Creative mode and then build what you learn into a game played on Survival.

Follow these steps to create an item sorter:

1. Start by placing two chests three blocks apart (see Figure 7.2). We'll use the first to store the items we want sorted, and the second to receive them.

2. Open the Creative inventory (press **E**) and switch to the **Buildcraft Pipes** tab on Page 2 of the inventory menu.

3. Select the first item, Wooden Transport Pipe: Extraction Pipe. Also collect a Cobblestone Transport Pipe.

4. Switch to the **Buildcraft Blocks** tab and get a Redstone Engine.

5. Pick up a wrench from the **Buildcraft Items** tab. The wrench is used to change the orientation of engines if they don't place the way you intended.

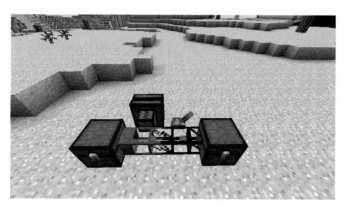

FIGURE 7.2 Creating the first BuildCraft transport pipe to shift objects from the chest on the left to the one on the right.

6. Pull a redstone lever from the inventory's **redstone** tab.

7. Collect a few other items to place in the chest. I'm going to use a full stack (64 blocks) of sand and a full stack of cobblestone. You can collect a stack by holding down the **Shift** key as you click the item. Place the stacks in the leftmost chest.

8. Place the wooden transport pipe on the block to the right of the leftmost chest. The pipe will connect automatically to the chest. Wooden pipes are a unique type of pipe that, when powered, can extract items from a block's inventory. However, they cannot connect to other wooden pipes, hence the need for the cobblestone pipe.

9. Place the cobblestone transport pipe in the block between the wooden pipe and the rightmost chest. It will connect to the wooden pipe and also to the chest. Cobblestone, like some of the other pipes, is used to transport items over long distances. It's the slowest of the lot, but also the easiest to make on Survival. These pipes can place items directly into a block's inventory, so you'll see it attach directly to the chest using a slightly different texture from the wooden pipe.

10. Place the redstone engine on the block behind the wooden pipe. You'll notice it orient itself correctly so that it directly faces the pipe. Engines always exhibit this behavior, although if there are multiple locations where the engine can attach, you may need to use the wrench to twist the engine around until it faces the correct pipe or device.

11. Place the redstone lever on the ground beside the engine, or attach it directly to the engine's back panel. Redstone engines are the least powerful of the three in BuildCraft, but also the easiest to use. However, they can generally only be used to power pipes and other very low-energy tasks. There is one other type of engine, the Creative Engine, so called because it is available only in Creative mode. It makes it easy to provide varying amounts of power to devices and systems.

12. Pull the lever to switch on the engine, and you'll start to see a stream of the blocks from the supply chest on the left move along the pipe into the second chest on the right.

Stop the lever after a few items have transferred and manually transfer the items from the second chest back to the first.

It's time to get things sorted! We'll do that with another type of pipe. Follow these steps while referring to Figure 7.3:

1. Add another chest in front of the second, with a space between so they don't convert into a single large chest.

2. Run a loop of cobblestone pipe out the front of the first piece to the new chest, as shown in the figure. The T-junction and pipe elbow are added automatically.

3. Pick up a Diamond Transport Pipe from the inventory and remove the T-junction of the first pipe. Attach a piece of the diamond pipe in its place.

   Diamond pipes act as sorters. When placed at a junction, they appear with different colored indicators for each of the six possible connections (left, right, top, bottom, front, and back). In Figure 7.3 you can see blue used for the pipe coming in from the supply chest, red for the one going into the chest to its right, and yellow for the branch leading to the new chest.

4. Grab any item besides a pipe and right-click the diamond T-junction to open the pipe's configuration window, shown in Figure 7.4, and place a block from your inventory on the appropriate color. I've chosen to send sand to the second chest and cobblestone to the third.

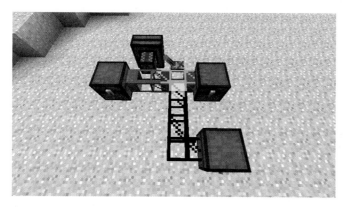

FIGURE 7.3 Pipes connect automatically, like redstone circuits, and some can implement a full range of logic control to the items passing through.

TIP

Filter Fixes

Pipes configured into a T-junction will send objects down both paths, even when a filter such as the diamond pipe has been used. Remember to set a specific filter on each outlet of a diamond pipe to block the flow of unwanted items.

5. Restock the supply chest with sand and cobblestone and pull the lever to restart the pipe. You should see the items hit the sorter and flow in the correct direction toward their respective chests.

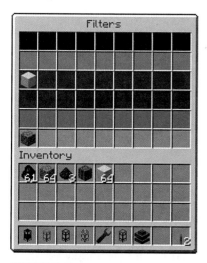

FIGURE 7.4 Place the filter blocks onto the colors corresponding with the directions shown on the diamond T-junction.

It's easy to expand this sorting system and to use it instead of the automatic sorter described in Chapter 6. Figure 7.5 shows one example.

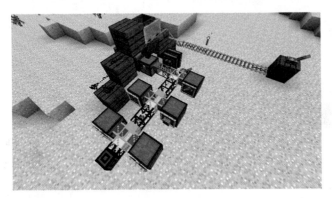

FIGURE 7.5 Automated produce sorter. The purple pipe at the end is a Void pipe that will destroy any extraneous items that aren't shuffled into the other chests.

BuildCraft provides a number of special-purpose pipes that can do everything but fold your laundry:

- **Void pipe**—As shown in Figure 7.5, this pipe destroys any items passed toward it.

- **Emerald pipe**—Similar to the wooden pipe, it can pull items from an object's inventory; however, it also contains a filter system with nine positions. By default, the pipe will only pull items included in the filter, but it can also be set to an excluding mode using the middle filter setting to pull all items except those in the filter, and it can also be set to a round-robin mode where one of each item shown in the filter is pulled in turn, stopping when any particular item runs out. This is a useful way to send a batch of items to a crafting table (see Figure 7.6).

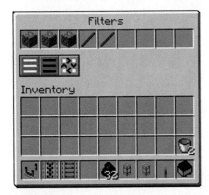

FIGURE 7.6 The emerald pipe's filter set to round-robin mode will supply each item placed in the filter in turn until one of the resources runs out. In this case, it's supplying sets of three cobblestone and two sticks for crafting a pickaxe.

- **Stripes pipe**—This pipe is very unusual. When powered, the end of the pipe will pick up any block placed in front of it. Figure 7.7 shows how this can be used to vacuum up the cobblestone created in a cobblestone generator and then feed the blocks through a cobblestone pipe directly into a chest. When unpowered, it will either place or use items. For example, it will place torches, levers, or even plant seeds. Send a pickaxe through and it will break the block in front. A hoe will turn a grass block into tilled dirt ready for planting. This opens up some interesting ideas for creating automated farms. Finally, sending a regular piece of transport pipe through lengthens the pipe to which the stripes pipe is attached, although because there is no way to also reduce the length of the pipe, this has somewhat limited potential.

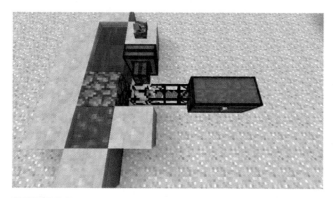

FIGURE 7.7 The stripes pipe will suck up blocks such as those created in this cobblestone generator.

- **Obsidian pipe**—These pipes suck up any loose items in front. Powering them with an engine increases the area's effect. Use these instead of hoppers to funnel drops from a mob farm into a chest, and to pick up harvested produce.

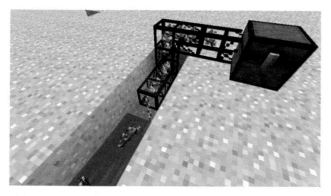

FIGURE 7.8 Obsidian pipes make it easy to collect item drops such as the wheat flowing down this stream.

There are also additional pipes for more complex transportation tasks, including the Emzuli pipe, which is used in conjunction with logic gates to paint items passing through for later routing.

Those are the basic concepts behind transportation pipes. Later on I take you on a tour of those that are used to transport fluids and power; you'll need to route water to the combustion engine to keep it cool, and also provide fuel.

Engines

As I mentioned earlier, BuildCraft has three basic types of engine, as well as a fourth that can be useful when playing in Creative mode:

- **Wooden engine**—This is the simplest type of engine. As you've already seen, powering a wooden engine requires nothing more than a redstone torch. However, the power output is so low at 0.5 MJ/t that it isn't useful for doing much at all except extracting objects from an inventory via the wooden extraction pipe.

- **Stirling engine**—This engine relies on a fuel source such as coal, charcoal, wood, sticks, or buckets of lava. It produces 1 MJ/t, sufficient for power mining wells and quarries.

- **Combustion engine**—The combustion engine relies on oil (producing 3 MJ/t) or oil refined into fuel (producing 6 MJ/t).

> ## NOTE
>
> ### Energy
>
> BuildCraft has, at its core, a concept of power similar to the redstone system but with substantially more finesse. Engines provide power, measured in Minecraft Joules per tick (MJ/t), whereas machines consume power at varying rates. Engines also store power in an internal buffer. Power is transferred from one area to another via kinesis pipes.

Engines can connect directly to the various BuildCraft machines, and also to each other to provide additional steps in power. However, due to a certain amount of energy loss when chaining, this only works with the stirling and combustion engines.

The stirling and combustion engines pose a risk of explosion (a significant one that can take out a large section of construction) if not correctly managed. Both must have some sort of work to do that will drain the energy they are producing; otherwise, they will overheat and explode. The combustion engine also requires water for cooling, or the same thing can happen.

Because engines require substantial resources to build and manage on Survival, it's a good idea to set them up as a small power station and then use kinesis pipes to distribute the energy where required. Let's do that now.

Creating a Power Station

Power stations are used to deliver energy to machines from a centralized source.

Given that some machines such as the quarry (discussed later) can use the power from nine combustion engines, and it takes care to set up and manage each combustion engine to prevent explosions, a single centralized power station makes sense.

Follow these steps to start creating your own. We'll start with the stirling engine and then create a more advanced design for combustion engines:

1. Place two rows of three stirling engines, as shown in Figure 7.9. This will provide up to 6 MJ/t of energy.

FIGURE 7.9 Stirling engines are twice as powerful as the wooden engine, providing 1 MJ/t of energy.

2. Run a row of blocks between the engines with redstone dust on top and a lever at one end, as shown in Figure 7.10. All of the BuildCraft engines only operate when they receive a redstone signal, so this lever will become the station's master switch.

3. Energy is extracted from engines with the wooden kinesis pipe. Select this from the inventory and right-click to place a single section on top of each engine. You'll notice from the tooltip in the inventory that each pipe section can handle a total energy throughput of 32 MJ/t—more than enough to handle the 1 MJ/t produced by each engine. However, these pipes are only used to connect to an energy producer and cannot connect to each other.

4. Select the cobblestone kinesis pipe from the inventory, right-click on top of each wooden section, and then place additional sections to link each engine to the one adjacent. You can do this in numerous ways. Figure 7.11 shows one example.

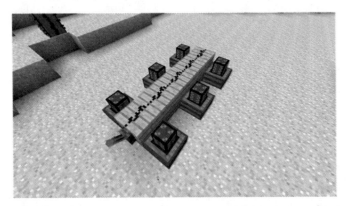

FIGURE 7.10 It's important to deliver a redstone signal to each engine. Using a lever provides a master switch, but you could also use a signal from some other component in your design that requests energy only when required.

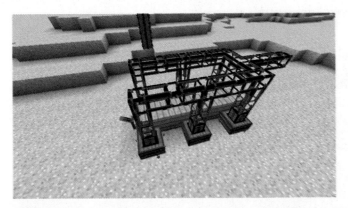

FIGURE 7.11 All BuildCraft's pipes connect automatically, so it takes just seconds to build up this entire framework. Energy from each row of engines is gathered at the T-junction located at the right of the structure, but connections can be made anywhere along the kinesis pipes.

5. Stirling engines can consume lava, coal, charcoal, and wood. Right-click each engine to open its interface and move a bucket of lava into the engine's fuel slot. Then flick the lever to power the station.

At this point the power station is producing energy, but it's not actually being used for anything. We'll connect it to a few things shortly. Meanwhile, let's ensure the station can fuel itself.

Although buckets of lava provide a long-lasting fuel source for stirling engines, they're not renewable in the way that something such as coal is. Switch off the power station and follow these steps:

1. Place a chest at the back of the power station with one space between it and the end of the run of redstone. We'll load this with coal.

2. Attach a wooden transport pipe to the back of the chest to pull out its contents and then place a wooden engine on top of the pipe (see Figure 7.12). It should automatically align itself so it's facing down. The engine can draw power from the redstone used to turn on the engines.

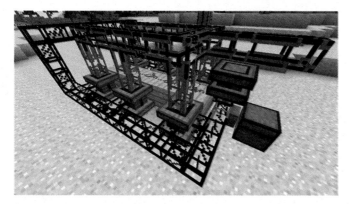

FIGURE 7.12   Setting up an automatic fuel feeder from a chest to each engine.

3. Run a cobblestone transport pipe around the engines and ensure they are connected to form a complete loop. Make an arch at the front if you want easier access to the lever.

4. Right-click each engine and remove the empty bucket from its fuel source. This makes room for coal.

5. Place six or so full stacks of coal in the chest and switch on the power station. You'll see the coal moving into the pipe, gradually making its way into the fueling stations of each engine. When the fuel stack of each engine is full, the coal will bypass it, and continue on its journey around the pipe until it finds a home.

Those are the basics of a stirling engine power station.

Combustion engines, especially those that rely on refined fuel, are significantly more complex. Let's put this first station to work and then look at the next.

Mining Wells

Mining wells work very simply: Give them a source of power and they'll quietly dig all the way to bedrock, only stopping if they hit lava on the way. Attach a chest or pipe to the side and they'll feed it the results. They'll even dig up diamonds, even though obsidian isn't required to build the device. Also, once you have one, you can run it until it stops and then collect it up with an iron, gold, or diamond pickaxe and reuse it again and again.

Start by grabbing a mining well from the Creative inventory and place it somewhere close to the power station. Then run a cobblestone kinesis pipe from the kinesis pipe at the front of the station into the side of the well.

Place a chest adjacent to the well and turn on the power station. Figure 7.13 shows the end result.

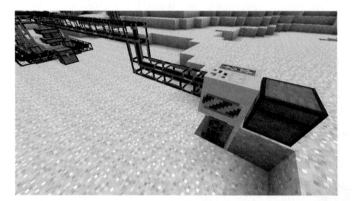

FIGURE 7.13 As soon as the mining well, or any device, starts drawing power, you'll see a laser-like cyan line running through the kinesis pipes.

NOTE

Multiplying Mining Wells

Add more than one mining well in a row, feeding into chests via pipes, to dig out additional ore; however, keep in mind that this won't increase the rate of ore recovery. The power from the station is evenly split between the wells, with each requiring an accumulation of 25 MJ to mine each block. Figure 7.14 shows a row of three wells. The one on the left side can deliver its results to a chest using one section of cobblestone pipe.

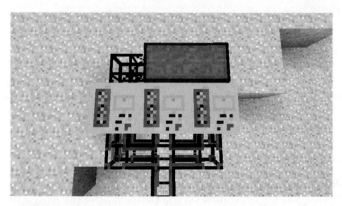

FIGURE 7.14 Running power to three mining wells and collecting the results in a chest.

TIP

Managing Power

Kinesis pipes carry a limited amount of power. You can see the maximum value in the tooltips, with the different types ranging from just 8 MJ for the cobblestone kinesis pipe to a whopping 1,024 MJ for the diamond version. View the current power output of an engine by right-clicking to open its inventory window, and then hover the mouse over the icon off to the right. You also see a visual indication of the energy output through the thickness of the blue line running along the middle of the pipe when the engine is in use. This will ultimately turn red when overloaded.

Avoid this by using a segment of iron kinesis pipe. Right-click it with a wrench to limit the maximum power that can enter the subsequent kinesis pipe.

If you are playing on Survival, you'll find that mining wells convert into pumps with the addition of a tank. We're going to need these to run combustion engines and take the power generation to the next level.

Managing Combustion Engines

Combustion engines are the most powerful in BuildCraft. They run on oil or fuel. Although you'll find deposits of oil and even the occasional oil geyser in a world created with the BuildCraft mod installed, you'll need to produce fuel by running oil through a refinery. Fuel tends to be far more efficient than oil, and produces more power.

Get started by locating an oil deposit. If you can't find one nearby, you can cheat on Creative by getting the oil spring block from the inventory and placing ten or so in a suitable location. Oil spring blocks convert to oil springs on a random basis, but it should only take a minute or two for you to start to see the first springs appear. Note that oil does not spring eternal. Each block is the equivalent of a bucket, and these can be pumped quite quickly, so locating a large deposit is better. (When you find one, jump in to see how deep it is. Although black on the surface, oil appears like water when you're submerged so you can easily see its extent.) You can also create your own deposit by repeatedly spilling the oil bucket into a depression in the ground.

You'll also need a nearby source of water that you can create with the water spring block, or just dig a hole that is 3×3 in width and length, and 1 block deep, and fill it with water from buckets. (Although a 2×2 hole creates an infinite water source, it may not refill quickly enough to supply the engines with sufficient cooling, so the 3×3 choice is safer.)

We'll create a power station composed of three combustion engines. Two stirling engines will power the pump to provide sufficient water, and a last one, just the regular wooden engine, will pump oil. If the engines run on oil, they'll provide a total of 9 MJ/t, but when running on fuel this increases to 18 MJ/t, so we'll also add a refinery later.

In Survival, pumps are crafted with a mining well and a tank, but stay in Creative for now. Follow these steps:

1. Place three combustion engines in a row, with a space between each. Then place a pump above one edge of the water supply, and another at the edge of the oil deposit, as shown in Figure 7.15.

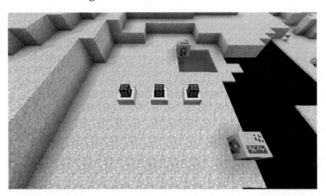

FIGURE 7.15 Initial layout of the combustion engine power station.

2. Use a stone fluid transport pipe to connect the oil pump to one side of each engine, and a gold fluid transport pipe to run water to the other side, as shown in Figure 7.16. I'm using gold for the water because it can transport four times as much liquid as stone, and it's vital to ensure sufficient water reaches the engines. You may find in some cases that you need to connect an output pipe to two sides of the pump to increase the pump's total capacity. Incidentally, there's no need to use a wooden fluid extraction pipe on pumps; they'll push liquid on their own into any connected fluid pipe. If you're building a more extensive power station, it can be important to ensure the same length of pipe reaches each engine from the water reservoir, ensuring each engine receives the same amount of fluid. Otherwise, the one at the end may not get enough and could overheat.

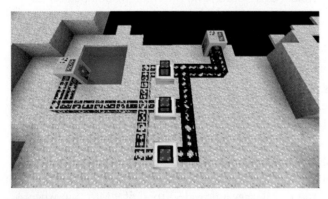

FIGURE 7.16 Running stone and gold pipes to the engines to provide coolant and oil.

3. As you did with the previous power station, place a wooden kinesis pipe segment on top of each engine, and link them across the top with a quartz kinesis pipe. Quartz kinesis pipes can carry up to 64 MJ/t, which will be sufficient for the power station's total output of 18 MJ/t.

4. Combustion engines run a grave risk of exploding, so we're going to add a logic gate that supplies the engine with a redstone signal only if it is in a blue or green condition. Any other power state indicates it is overheating, so it should be turned off to give it time to cool. Get an iron OR gate from the inventory and place it against each wooden kinesis pipe segment. You should end up with something like what's shown in Figure 7.17.

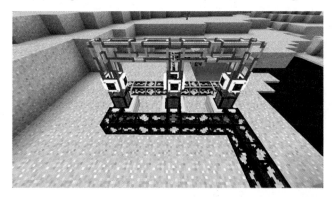

FIGURE 7.17   The station after the iron OR logic gate is added.

5. Right-click each gate to open its configuration window. Click the four boxes until you have the configuration shown in Figure 7.18. The gate's logic says that when the engine is blue or green, supply a redstone signal to the surrounding blocks (which includes the engine), thus turning it on.

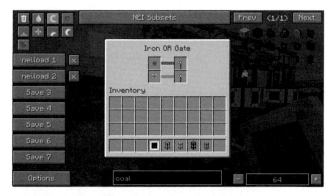

FIGURE 7.18   Configuring the iron OR gate.

6. Place a stirling engine behind the water pump and a wooden engine behind the oil pump. You can power them with levers or torches, or run redstone back to a central point, as shown in Figure 7.19.

TIP

Plugging Up Pipes

Most pipes automatically connect to others, so running them in tight configurations can prove something of a challenge. You can use pipe plugs to prevent fluids from commingling. Just apply a plug or plugs to the surface of a pipe where it would otherwise connect and you'll be able to run the other pipe safely alongside. Stone and cobblestone pipes don't connect, so they provide a good option for running different fluids side by side.

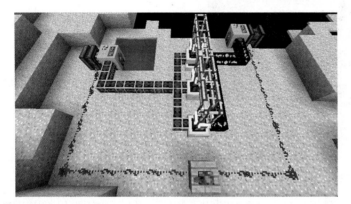

FIGURE 7.19 Combustion engine power station finalized.

Now that you have all that power, it's time to do something with it. For a quick test, try extending the stone kinesis pipe to a mining well. You'll see blocks flying out of the ground at a far greater rate than with the stirling power station.

However, we want to get even more power from this set up, and for that we need to create a refinery and then supply the engines with fuel. This will double the power output.

TIP

Getting Pumped About Oil

Over time, power stations can deplete any but the largest oil reserves. Fortunately, you'll more than likely find extensive reserves underground, especially after you dig out large sections using the quarry mining machine. You can bring these up with a pump. It actually doesn't matter how deep they are: The pump will stretch down. Then either feed them directly into your current oil pipes or use the flood gate machine to spill the oil back into the main reserve.

Refining Oil

Refineries convert oil into fuel. Although fuel is only used by combustion engines, it produces twice as much power, and lasts five times as long, producing 250,000 MJ per bucket, lasting 40 minutes, compared to oil's 25,000 MJ and 8 minutes of runtime.

Place a refinery on the oil side of the power station next to the current oil pipe. Then run a quartz kinesis pipe from the power station's kinesis line to the refinery, as shown in Figure 7.20.

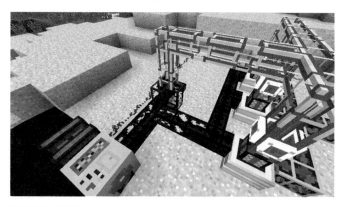

FIGURE 7.20 Refineries use energy to convert oil into the far more efficient fuel.

Refineries are composed of three tanks. Two hold oil while the last holds the fuel. The refinery will gradually fill up this last tank.

Let the refinery run for a few minutes to fill this up, then break the oil pipe running to the engines and replace it with a fresh stone pipe that connects to the front of the refinery with a wooden fluid extraction pipe.

Place a wooden engine beside the pipe and power it with a torch or by connecting it to the redstone line. See Figure 7.21 for my version.

FIGURE 7.21 Replumbing the power station to operate on the fuel produced by the refinery.

When each engine has used up its oil, it will take in the fuel and increase its power output to 6 MJ/t.

And there you have it: a safe combustion power station.

Automated Quarries

Now that you have a solid source of power, let's put it to good use.

The quarry is one of the most powerful features of BuildCraft. Think of it like the mining well on steroids.

In its standard mode it will dig a 9×9 hole in the ground all the way to bedrock or lava, whichever comes first, but by using landmarks (something I'll introduce shortly), it's possible to create a quarry up to an enormous 64×64 blocks.

Figure 7.22 shows the simplest possible quarry: the quarry block, a chest to collect the results, and a stirling engine. Placing the quarry block also creates the black and yellow striped frame. The quarry first destroys any blocks inside the frame, as shown by the red blocks flying out of the machine. It then constructs a frame and will start to dig, as shown in Figure 7.23.

FIGURE 7.22 A basic quarry in its construction phase.

FIGURE 7.23 Stirling engines provide only minimal power to a quarry, so a setup such as this digs quite slowly.

Start your own quarry reasonably close to the power station so that you don't need to run the power too far. Accessing the power from the station will provide the quarry with sufficient power to run at a good trot. Follow these steps to create a custom-sized quarry:

1. BuildCraft's landmark tool makes it easy to define a larger area. Place landmarks at each corner of the area you want to mine. They must be on the same level and aligned perfectly, but there's an easy way to do this. Place the landmark in the first corner and then put a redstone torch beside it to make a set of handy guidelines appear, as shown in Figure 7.24.

FIGURE 7.24 It doesn't take any more resources to create a quarry machine that is much larger than the standard 9X9 square. Just use landmarks to define the size.

2. Follow the blue guidelines, placing landmarks at each corner along with another torch to form new guidelines. The guidelines can go through other blocks and appear on the other side. If you find an intended corner is underground, dig down and place the landmark once you see the intersection.

3. Right-click one of the landmarks to make the area active. You'll see it change to a red square.

4. Place the quarry block directly behind the landmark that is nearest the power station. It shouldn't be inside or resting on the red square. If you've done this correctly, the black and yellow striped frame will appear, matching the dimensions of the red square.

6. Place a chest beside the quarry block to collect the results, then connect the quarry to the power station with quartz kinesis pipe and watch it spring into action (see Figure 7.25).

Quarries dig up a lot of material, and you may not want to save all that sand, dirt, and cobblestone. The easiest way to deal with this is to use stone transport pipes connected to chests. Use a diamond transport pipe at each junction to sort the items you do want to keep (even with multiple chests such as those shown in Figure 7.26), and then use a section of void transport pipe at the end to destroy the unwanted blocks. Remember to use actual diamonds, emeralds, redstone, and coal instead of their ore blocks in the filters because the quarry delivers the same results that you do by mining. All other results are delivered as ore.

FIGURE 7.25 The finished quarry in action. Yep, that's a big hole in the ground.

FIGURE 7.26 A diamond pipe sorting system to ensure the best results from the quarry are saved and the rest discarded.

The power station provides more than enough juice to run more than one quarry at a time. Place another beside the first, staking it out with landmarks, and use an iron routing pipe to connect it to the output of the first quarry. (Use the spanner tool if the pipe doesn't orient correctly right away and blocks pop out.) Figure 7.27 shows an example.

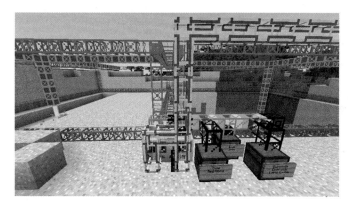

FIGURE 7.27 Add a second quarry beside the first. Split the power before it reaches the first quarry to ensure both receive the same amount.

Blueprints, Building, and Templates

Ever built a house or other kind of structure and thought, that's awesome, but making it again is going to be a serious pain? Or maybe you saw someone else's house on a multiplayer server and figure you'd like to borrow the design for your own world?

With BuildCraft, this is astonishingly easy. On Survival it's not a cheat as such: You'll still need to gather all the required resources. However, it does vastly simplify the re-creation of structures. Actually, even most of the power plant is easily re-created almost in its entirety, although a few blocks are missing.

The design is stored as a blueprint or template and can be stored and shared between players. See the upcoming tip "Sharing Is Caring" for more.

Here's how it works:

1. Use landmarks to define the base of the area you want to copy.

2. Place a further landmark above one of the corners to define the height of the area. The landmarks can be placed vertically or against the side of a surface. If you need to, build a temporary pillar to gain height.

3. Right-click one of the base landmarks to form a rectangle, then do the same to the top landmark to turn the area into a three-dimensional box. In Figure 7.28 I'm copying the design of the village smithy's workshop.

4. Place an architect table directly behind one of the landmarks to convert the area into the yellow-and-black frame you've seen previously with the quarry.

5. Right-click the table to open the window shown in Figure 7.29. Type in a name and then drop a blank blueprint or template into the input box. Blueprints store the specific object types required to re-create a design. Templates store just the shape, which can then be filled with any type of block from your inventory.

FIGURE 7.28 Defining the area to copy.

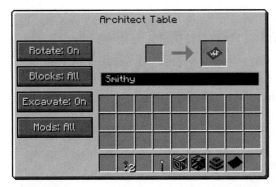

FIGURE 7.29 Creating a blueprint of the smithy workshop.

TIP

Explosive Templates

Because templates provide a way to copy any existing design and then replace the structure with blocks of your choice, you might as well have some fun. Try copying your current house into a template, move a safe distance away, place a builder machine, and then re-create it from TNT. How long can you resist setting it off with a flint and steel?

6. Take the printed blueprint and head to the area you want to re-create the design.

7. Place a builder machine facing in the direction you want to build. It will build from the same corner the blueprint was created. Right-click it to open the window shown in Figure 7.30.

8. Drag the blueprint to the input box at the top and you'll see all the resources required in the area to the right. Match these by dragging the resources from your inventory into the builder's inventory. There's no need to include items that you don't require. For example, this blueprint has also taken a copy of all the items in the smithy's chest, but I'll just leave those behind. By the way, before you copy those in, you may want to exit the builder and check that the outline of the area that's shown extending from the builder has the design positioned where you desire.

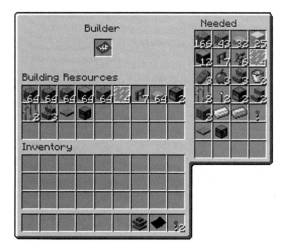

FIGURE 7.30 Matching the resources required by the blueprint. In Creative you can actually just activate the builder without having the resources in place.

9. When you're ready, place a stirling engine beside the builder and power it up. Presto! The builder will get to work re-creating the original design (see Figure 7.31).

FIGURE 7.31 The completed auto-constructed smithy building.

TIP

Sharing Is Caring

The BuildCraft Library is a special block that stores blueprints and templates for easy retrieval. Place a printed blueprint or template to permanently store it, and feed it a blank blueprint or template to take a copy of any stored design. BuildCraft libraries are a perfect way to share builds on multiplayer servers—everything from houses to decorative items (a fancy fountain or statue), to farms and even redstone machines. You'll find a large collection of blueprints at http://www.mod-buildcraft.com. Download them as per usual and copy them to a folder called "blueprints," stored under your *Minecraft* application. Restart *Minecraft* and place a library to access the files. (You'll need to reload *Minecraft* each time you copy a new blueprint to the folder to see it appear in the library.)

More BuildCraft

There's a lot more to BuildCraft besides what's described in this chapter. Here are some of the more fascinating features:

- **Advanced logic gates**—Automatically shut down engines and machinery depending on the work required and available resource, or build complex routing logic. Autarchic gates replace the need for extraction pipes to be powered with engines. Gates are constructed with wire and chipsets, and all three can be crafted automatically on an assembly table powered by lasers. Yes, that's right, lasers.

- **Pipe wire**—Each pipe segment can support up to four strands of wire to enable the transmission of signals. The wires won't lattice like regular redstone, making it easy to route multiple signals and then respond to them with gates.

- **Pipe facades**—Don't want to look like you're living in an oil refinery? Hide your pipes with facades that match the surrounding material. Phased facades can even switch between two materials depending on the status of an underlying pipe wire, thus providing a useful visual signal.

- **Automatic crafting table**—This table works like a regular crafting table but includes an inventory for storing item components. Connect pipes to the table to build items and move them elsewhere. Use multiple crafting tables linked in this way to build an assembly line, shuffling completed items from one table to the next so they become part of the next recipe. It's a factory in a box. The advanced crafting table is similar, but provides an inventory for the output.

■ **Filler machine**—The filler creates prototypical shapes in a defined area using whatever materials are provided to its inventory. Build a giant pyramid or a hollow box for your next power station. Or just fill in those giant holes created by your quarries.

The Bottom Line

BuildCraft is a fabulous mod that changes the nature of the game. Played on Survival, there is a significant challenge in gathering the resources to create the various devices and supporting structures. It defines an ambitious series of goals. But even on Creative there is something deeply satisfying in creating a self-sustaining power station that doesn't explode. In fact, something you can try now is to double the size of the current design to six combustion engines. You can run them in sequence or flip the design to mirror it on the other side of the current design.

Some information on BuildCraft is available online that will also help, although it isn't necessarily up to date. Try these sites for more information:

■ Visit the official website at http://www.mod-buildcraft.com.

■ If you've installed BuildCraft as part of the Tekkit mod pack, you can also find additional information at http://goo.gl/N1BXK7.

■ There's also a handy, if somewhat dated, tutorial at http://goo.gl/DlAFRZ.

■ A future version of BuildCraft already in development adds robots that can automatically chop wood, kill mobs, mine, plant, and much more. Check the official website at http://www.mod-buildcraft.com for more details.

In the next chapter we're going to explore a mod that goes even deeper than BuildCraft in some very interesting ways (forget combustion—let's go nuclear!). Like other mods such as the Forestry plugin (http://forestry.sengir.net), it was designed for compatibility with BuildCraft, allowing pipes, energy, crafting tables, and other items to interact with its own systems.

Titans of IndustrialCraft

In This Chapter

- Become of a captain of industry.
- Plant a seed and understand the new agriculture.
- Crossbreed plants to create iron and gold farms.
- Upscale your armor like never before.
- Create an EU generator, recharge batteries, and run new mining machines.
- Thermonuclear engineering: It's fun for all the family.

IndustrialCraft[2] (IC2) introduces an amazing number of machines, energy sources, and concepts to *Minecraft*. It is, indeed, one of the largest mods in existence.

Even better, it's also compatible with a large number of other mods, and is often extended by those mods to improve compatibility. For example, the GregTech mod is almost as large as IC2, adds dozens of new machines, ores, and energy sources, and even increases IC2's compatibility with BuildCraft.

The sheer extent of this mod means it's not possible to cover it in one chapter (it could easily take up an entire book on its own); however, you will learn its core concepts and build some rather cool systems, weapons, and tools, and even develop new plant species.

Before we get started, it should be noted that IC2 has become IndustrialCraft[2] Experimental (or, as I use herein, IC2E), available from http://goo.gl/AwJSFS. This is an in-progress redevelopment of IC2 and subject to large-scale changes, so keep your hardhat on, and don't be too alarmed if a few things here and there have changed by the time you try it out.

IC2E Core Concepts

Like BuildCraft, the IC2E mod requires Forge. It's currently updated for *Minecraft* v1.7.10. You'll also find it much easier to use with the Not Enough Items (NEI) mod, which shows the various crafting recipes.

IC2E adds some interesting goals to *Minecraft*, not least the ability to build jetpacks, mining lasers, and even a nuclear power station. They're all bundled under an additional tab in the Creative menu, as shown in Figure 8.1. The key elements are as follows:

- **Agriculture**—Consider this the vanilla crops system completely reimagined. There are many more types of crops, as well as the ability to crossbreed plant species to achieve particular advantages. But be warned: You'll also need to cope with nefarious weeds.

- **Armor**—Fancy being able to leap tall buildings in a single bound, and avoid breaking your ankles on the way down? The Quantum and NanoSuits are just what you need. Combine them with a jetpack to achieve extended flight.

- **Energy and Wiring**—IC2E has its own energy units (EU) that are also used extensively across its add-on mods. Generators produce EU in varying amounts, while wires and machines can explode if fed too much. The amount of EU produced by by generators ranges from 8 EU/t (solar panel, water mill, and windmill) to 2 billion EU/t (fusion reactor and supercondensator). Given that so many of this mod's tools and devices rely on EU, it's important to set up a proper generation facility. I'll show you how later in this chapter.

- **Ingots, Blocks, and Plates**—IC2E introduces many new ores, such as bronze, copper, lead, and tin (perfect for extracting with one of BuildCraft's automated quarries, or IC2E's own miner machine). The ores are formed in various ways into the blocks, plates, and item casings needed to build additional items.

- **Machines**—There are an extraordinary number of machines in IC2E, including those for creating and storing energy, replicating advanced items, processing ores, forming metal components, analyzing circuits, teleporting, setting up nuclear reactors, and a lot more.

- **Tools**—Tired of your tools wearing down? Swap them for electrically powered ones, and then create advanced versions such as the powerful mining laser.

Let's start with the agricultural component and then get into some of the more advanced devices—although if you think this is just about some more boring farming, be warned: It takes the concept to a whole new level. As with the previous chapters on mods, I'd recommend you start on Creative to get an understanding for how things work, and then switch to a Survival game to build up from scratch. And remember, with NEI installed you can, even on Survival, press **R** with any item selected in its extended catalog to view the crafting recipe.

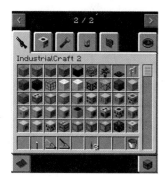

FIGURE 8.1   Just a fraction of the tools and other elements added to the game by IndustrialCraft[2] Experimental. (Note, also, the BuildCraft tabs from Chapter 7, "Empire Building with BuildCraft." These two mods play well together.)

Agricultural Pursuits

Add some color to your farm, and many other fruits from your labors, by crossbreeding to create new, hardy plant species. There are quite a few, but the following are key:

- **Reed**—Obtained from two sugar cane (or, less likely, two wheat), reed acts as the kick starter for stickreed, which, in turn, leads to the other crops.

- **Stickreed**—Produces sticky resin that can replace the slimeball required for sticky pistons. Actually, it can even be used in crafting torches instead of coal or charcoal. Sticky resin also oozes from the rubber trees that crop up in the swamp, taiga, and jungle biomes. Right-click the sap hole on a rubber tree while holding a treetap (see Figure 8.2) to extract resin in a renewable way, and then use a regular furnace or an extractor to convert that into rubber to insulate wires and prevent explosions from crossed connections. Rubber comes up in many crafting recipes, so ensuring a steady supply is important.

- **Ferru**—Provides a way to grow iron... yes, you heard that right. Harvesting ferru produces piles of iron dust that smelt back into iron ore. Always plant ferru on dirt with an iron ore block one or two blocks below. Use a quarry or miner to pull up iron ore from a large expanse and then place it down as a platform with the dirt on top, and you will eventually have yourself an iron farm that is substantially easier to create than trying to summons iron golems. Crossbreed ferru from two stickreed or a couple of terra wart.

- **Aurelia**—When planted on dirt with gold ore beneath, aurelia can produce gold nuggets. Grow by crossbreeding ferru with ferru, using a block of gold on top of one of iron, then dirt, to ensure a crossbreed of either aurelia or ferru has the opportunity to mature.

FIGURE 8.2   A set of three rubber wood trees. Note the two sticky resin tapping positions at the base of the middle tree. These can be tapped over and over, but only do so when they are orange and not black to avoid destroying them.

- **Coffee**—Used to harvest coffee beans, which, when turned into coffee powder, make a cup of the caffeinated stuff that provides the effects of the speed and haste potions. Brew coffee by grinding the beans in a macerator and then combining the powder with water and a stone mug. Produce with two stickreed or two terra wart.

- **Redwheat**—Produces redstone dust and wheat. Create with two aurelia or two nether wart.

- **Terra wart**—Removes poison effects in a similar way to drinking milk. Crossbreed from two stickreed, a pair of roses, or a couple of nether wart.

- **Hops**—Used to brew beer, which, while providing a boost to strength and damage resistance, also causes a range of negative effects such as mining fatigue, slowness, and nausea. Consuming terra wart solves the ills while leaving you with the benefits. (If only such things were true in real life.) Use two nether wart or a couple of stickreeds to create.

TIP

Ensuring Crops Mature

It's impossible to tell which crops are which at their early stage of growth because each tends to look like an already standard crop. For example, both ferru and aurelia have the same initial appearance. Build a Cropnalyzer as soon as possible (discussed later) to determine the type of plant and other useful crossbreeding statistics.

Crossbreeding Guide

Planting, growing, and crossbreeding introduces a few new requirements to the usual *Minecraft* procedure:

- Crops grow on an item called a *crop*—confusing, I know—crafted from four sticks and placed onto tilled soil. Think of it as a garden stake. To save confusion, I'll just call it a *wooden crop*. The usual rules for irrigation and light-levels apply.

- Place a second wooden crop in the same space as the first to create a crossbreeding block. As long as there are crops already growing on single wooden crop blocks on each side, this block has a chance of developing a crossbred crop. These usually share some attributes with the parent crops, but the results can be unusual. For example, you may find cocoa coming from wheat. In other cases, you'll receive one of IC2E's unique additions. Use a Cropnalyzer to discover the attributes of the crop and replant it if it's better than one you already have. This way, you gradually improve the growth rates and overall yield of your crops.

- Right-click a mature crop to harvest any drops without destroying the plant. Left-click it, but only in Survival mode, to remove the plant and gain the harvest and also, potentially, a seed bag that can be used to plant a new crop that could be an improved version of the original.

- Weeds will grow where the harvested crop once stood and can quickly spread, knocking out other plants. You'll need to keep a close eye on the crop or apply Weed-Ex in just the right amount so it doesn't also damage the plants. A Crop-Matron solves this.

- Plant *Minecraft*'s standard wheat, pumpkin, melon, and cocoa seeds directly on blocks with a single wooden crop added to each patch of tilled soil. They will grow within that single block and drop their fruit on harvesting. This allows for significantly more compact melon, pumpkin, and cocoa farms.

- The biome matters because it impacts hydration, which also affects the crop's rate of growth. Although this may be overcome with the Crop-Matron (she's coming up soon), the better the initial biome the fewer resources the Crop-Matron will use in keeping it properly hydrated. The best hydrated is the swamp, and then jungle, forest, and plains. Taiga and desert are the least kindly.

- Air quality, or the amount of space above the crop, matters in its growth rate and bio-logical diversity. Generally 10 or so blocks will do, so the open air works just fine, but even an overhanging leaf block from a tree can prevent any crop spawning.

Two designs work well for cross-breeding: the strip farm and the square farm.

Strip Farming for Profit

The strip farm is probably the one with which you are most familiar. It isn't the best design for crop farming because harvesting requires walking across the farmland, but it works. Follow these steps:

1. Place a water source and then extend out into a string of three tilled blocks. Place the wooden crop sticks in the first and second position and add a torch on the end to provide good growth conditions at night, as shown in Figure 8.3.

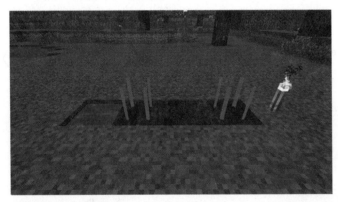

FIGURE 8.3   A starter design for crossbreeding. Swamp biomes provide the best farmland, but watch out for witches.

2. Plant a crop, preferably sugarcane under each wooden crop, then add a double set of wooden crops with two right-clicks to the middle block to turn it into the crossbreeding block, but don't plant a crop there. We want to see what springs up (see Figure 8.4).

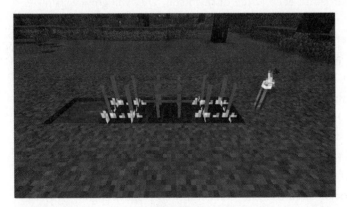

FIGURE 8.4   Note the sugarcane in its first stage of growth, surrounding each of the four wooden crop sticks on its block.

TIP

Leave Double Crops Until Last

You can help avoid weed infections by leaving the placement of the double crops to the centerline until after the surrounding crops mature.

3. The outer crops must grow to full maturity before there is any chance a crop will make its first tentative appearance in the crossbreeding block. As with all potential parents, this may take some time. While you wait, extend the design out four blocks on either side of the initial layout. I also put a fence around the farm with a few light sources for good measure. In Figure 8.5, you can see that a crop has appeared in the first section laid out in the middle. Creating a string of these crossbreeding sections nine blocks long greatly improves the possibility of getting a useful crossbreed. In this case, we're hoping for reed as a starting point for many a new species.

FIGURE 8.5 Sugar cane crossbreeds starting to appear. Once they've matured, they'll be gathered and examined.

4. Give it a while longer for the rest to appear. Ensure you are playing in Survival mode (type **/gamemode survival** if you need to) and then head up the middle of the field, left-clicking to pull up the plants themselves in the hope of getting seed drops. Figure 8.6 shows the final field with two obviously new crops.

5. All the collected drops include a combination of seed bags and actual produce, to one extent or another. The only problem for now is that the seed types are not known, although you can deduce some if they drop a crop such as carrots or cocoa. Just check the inventory each time you collect a crossbred crop. If you also get carrots or cocoa, the seed bag should belong to them, so arrange them beside each other in the inventory. If the crop comes up as unknown, with no drops, it's more than likely the sought-after reed. Group them separately. By the way, the Cropnalyzer does determine crop types, but you also need a source of power. I cover this topic separately later in the chapter.

6. Place a new wooden crop up the middle of the strip to turn the existing ones back into double crops; then replace the outer crops with the reed seeds, arranged in pairs, and let the crop cycle begin its circle of life.

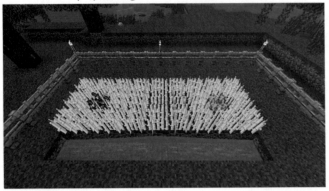

FIGURE 8.6   Early results look promising with two obviously different crops and the rest yet to be determined.

7. Repeat steps 4 to 6 with the next generation. You may be lucky enough to pick up sticky resin, indicating the seed bag holds the stickreed. From there you can pick up ferru, but ensure you place iron ore two blocks under their dirt blocks. After ferru you can get aurelia, adding a gold ore block just above the iron ore blocks so that the crossbreeding can deliver one or the other.

That's the general process. It seems involved but can move ahead quite quickly. On the first harvest I obtained one carrot seed bag, two cocoa, and seven reed. The next run delivered two stickreeds and six more reed, allowing the farm to quickly expand to another three rows of potential stickreed. Just stick with it and you'll quickly begin moving through the different crops.

CAUTION

Weeding Them Out

As crossbreeding continues, there's also an increasing risk weeds will raise their ugly heads. You can recognize them as a green X pattern hugging the lower half of the double crop sticks. Pull them out quick as you can to prevent them from spreading, and right-click the block with some Weed-Ex in hand. In the section "Improving Growth with a Crop-Matron," I explain how to handle these little suckers automatically.

Before we move onto the Cropnalyzer, let's take a look at another farm design.

Square Farm Dancing

The square farm is highly efficient because it allows up to four crossbreeds for every four seeds. Figure 8.7 shows the essential idea: Create farmland surrounding a water block and then place single wooden crops at the cardinal points in the middle of each border. Continue per Figure 8.8, placing double crops at each corner and planting four seed bags on the single crops placed earlier.

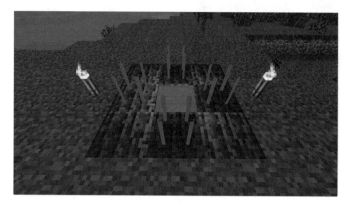

FIGURE 8.7   It's a square dance with a difference: an alternative and efficient farm layout.

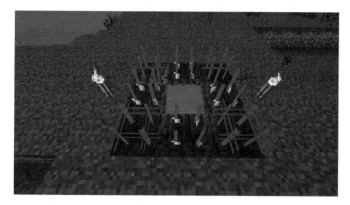

FIGURE 8.8   Turning each seed crop into a potential crossbreed.

The design is perfect for building out in an ongoing square pattern with pathways in between to enable easy harvesting. You'll find some of the harvest falling into the water in the middle. Dig tunnels underneath to create a central point that brings all those drops together, and then have that flow down to a funnel and chest for automatic collection (see Figure 8.9).

FIGURE 8.9   A 4×4 version of the square pattern with a central collection point.

Using the Cropnalyzer

The Cropnalyzer opens up the strategic portion of the IC2E agricultural system by unveiling a seed bag's characteristics.

It instantly identifies unknown seed bags and their DNA, and from there you can figure out the right crops to crossbreed and also at what point the crossbreeding has reached its useful limit. Figure 8.10 shows the device in action.

FIGURE 8.10   Analyze this: the DNA of a seed.

The goal is to set up different crops under optimal conditions to produce an improved mutation.

The Cropnalyzer gives you the information you need to control the process as best as possible, although the outcome is always somewhat random. Follow these steps:

1. Place a power source in the top-right slot of the Cropnalyzer. Just pull a charged RE-Battery from the Creative inventory. Performing the full four scans uses up the entire power of a fully charged RE-Battery. Figure 8.11 shows a simple-but-effective battery recharger that

takes just a few minutes to power up an RE-Battery. The Advanced RE-Battery provides 10 times as much power as the standard version, so it's a good choice if you need to scan a lot of seed bags, but in Survival will take significantly more effort to build.

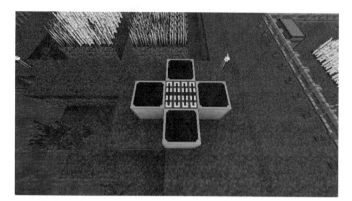

FIGURE 8.11   A simple battery charger: four Solar Panels and a BatBox. Right-click the BatBox and place an empty battery in the upper-left slot. Hover over it with the mouse to see its charging status, or just check the small status bar built into its icon.

2. Place the seed in the top-left slot. It transfers to the slot just to its right, and the first of four levels of information will appear. This information is stored with the seed bag, appears in tooltips in the inventory window, and also transfers to the crop where it appears with a right-click of the Cropnalyzer for no additional energy cost.

3. Transfer the seed bag back to the top-left slot to perform the next scan. You'll eventually see a full panel of information.

Each scan uncovers another layer of information:

- **Scan 1: Crop Name**—Probably the most important identifier at the start of a crossbreeding program.

- **Scan 2: Tier**—These range from 1 to 8 and are defined by the type of crop. For example, pumpkin and wheat are Tier 1, reed and melon are Tier 2, and so on. Always crossbreed crops that are no more than one tier apart. Incidentally, you'll also see the name of the developer who originally created the crop while working on this mod, or "Notch" if it's in vanilla *Minecraft*.

- **Scan 3: Keywords**—The keywords provide clues as to which crops are best to crossbreed together to obtain that particular crop. As long as both parental candidates are no more than one tier apart and share at least one keyword, they'll prove a good match.

- **Scan 4: Characteristics**—This is the most important aspect and also the most costly in terms of energy, but it is, after all, the point of crossbreeding. You'll see the following key measures of that seed bag's capabilities:

- **Growth**—This is the rate at which the plant matures and crossbreeds. The downside is that there's a commensurate increase in the rate at which weeds may break out, and at values above 24 the plant becomes itself like a weed, or even a Triffid, wiping out other crops. Keep it a few steps below that for optimum performance. This value is shown as **Gr** in tooltips.

  - **Gain**—Want more drops? Increase this number but beware that a value above 23 will cause the rate of seed bag drops to decrease. This value is shown as **Ga** in tooltips.

- **Resist**—Improves the hardiness of the plant against weeds, trampling, and generally poor conditions, such as a lack of hydration, but limits its ability to crossbreed with other crops at levels about 27. This value is shown as **Re** in tooltips.

So how do you best improve your crops? Combine them using the recommendations at the start of the chapter to develop new crops. But also crossbreed crops of the same type, and scan the results to compare them against similar types. If you discover the result has better characteristics than one or both of your current breeding pair, replace the worst of those with the new crop and continue crossbreeding.

Improving Growth with a Crop-Matron

The Crop-Matron is an advanced machine that automatically provides a huge square of 9×9 crops with fertilizer, hydration, and Weed-Ex, and does so at the optimal levels. It looks at all blocks on its current level, as well as one above and one below, providing flexibility in placement (see Figure 8.12).

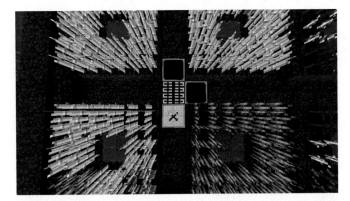

FIGURE 8.12 A Crop-Matron at ground-level, powered by a BatBox fed by two Solar Panels. This provides sufficient power for it to operate continuously day and night, keeping the four beds properly whipped into shape.

A Crop-Matron requires just 1 EU of power, which is something a Solar Panel is perfectly capable of delivering during the day, but cannot do at night. Two panels charging a BatBox will help it keep operating day and night, and three panels also sees it through periods of inclement weather.

To create this configuration, place the BatBox first, ensuring you're at its level so that its outlet (the white dot) faces the location the Crop-Matron should go. (If not, it won't supply the power. You can adjust its orientation with a wrench if things go awry.) Then add the Solar Panels.

Right-click the Crop-Matron to open the window shown in Figure 8.13. Add Fertilizer (to speed maturation and crossbreeding), Hydration Cells (making up for poor biomes), and Weed-Ex (killer of weeds) to its slots, as shown. Fertilizer is stackable up to 64 units, whereas the others take three units a piece and show their remaining capacity as they slowly empty. As with almost all the devices in IC2E, the Crop-Matron is compatible with BuildCraft pipes, so it's easy to resupply it from another inventory such as a chest or automatic crafting table.

FIGURE 8.13   The Crop-Matron in action... fighting for peace.

IC2E Armor, Weapons, and Tools

Let it be said: Once you've donned IC2E armor, you'll never want to go back to the vanilla *Minecraft* variety—not even when made of glittering diamonds. And forget the enchanted Sword of Smite III.

Let's take a look at the options:

- **Armor**—IC2E adds three varieties of armor: Bronze, Nano, and Quantum. The first performs like regular armor, but the second and third are electrically powered. As long as you keep them charged up, you'll have full protection without ever losing protection. Quantum boots also protect you from all fall damage, even if you've flown to the top of the world in a jetpack and plummeted hundreds of blocks in a reverse swan dive. They'll even protect you from the blast of an exploding nuclear reactor from just four blocks away.

- **Weapons**—Although bronze weapons make an appearance, the Mining Laser is a fun projectile weapon for attacking from a distance, even if it doesn't cause a lot of damage. And you may want a NanoSaber because it's the only weapon that can make mincemeat of a NanoSuit.

■ **Tools**—Herein lies a feast o' plenty. Electrical tools never lose durability, and although the diamond mining drill and electric chainsaw are not quite as fast as their regular diamond counterparts, they'll keep running forever with a little power topping them up. Other helpers such as the OD and OV Scanners provide an instant analysis of the number and type of valuable ores in a 5×5 or 9×9 area directly beneath your feet, as shown in Figure 8.14. (The scanners also work with the automatic miners in IC2E to dig ores out of the same size area while leaving other blocks in place, so scanning first, then placing the scanner in a miner tells you in advance exactly what you'll get. Like a nervous dentist, you never need fear drilling in the wrong place again.)

FIGURE 8.14 Like an MRI for mining, the OD and OV Scanners can show you the best places to drill.

Although none of these items are so complex as to require instructions on use, here are a few key pointers:

■ A BatPack storing 60,000 EU handily recharges most of the portable electrical tools for a very long time. If not, a LapPack (an upgraded version storing 300,000 EU) will definitely do the job. Wear them instead of a chest plate to recharge your tools. Alternatively, carry batteries with you, select them from a hotbar slot, and hold down a right-click to charge up any tools in your inventory.

■ The Electric Jetpack can fly just about forever if you wear a Solar Helmet, but only in clear daylight weather. Make sure you don't get stuck without power while flying across a ravine, or deep in a cave; otherwise, you'll plummet like Icarus. Put on the jetpack like you would chest plate armor and take it off by holding down the spacebar.

■ Right-click while holding the NanoSaber to turn it on and off.

■ Right-click while holding an Electric Drill to place torches from your inventory. This makes exploring and mining fast and convenient. You can get in and out before the hostile mobs even notice you're there.

■ Some of the tools such as the Mining Laser have different modes (see Figure 8.15). Hold down the mode shift key (by default **M**, and right-click with the tool in hand). If you are using REI's MiniMap, which also defaults to **M**, you may want to change its key configuration to something else, or use *Minecraft*'s control options to map the mode shift key to **Z**.

FIGURE 8.15 Feeling scattershot? Try that mode with the mining laser and fling out a spray of red energy.

■ Mining deep in a cave system with a jetpack and electric drill makes things ridiculously easy. Ravines and deep caves no longer present the slightest problem—unless, of course, you run out of power. Oops!

Although these IC2E additions to *Minecraft* completely change the game, in some cases they require materials that can only be made in other machines, and they all need recharging at various levels. Doing so without waiting all day takes generators that can produce power at 10 times that of solar panels.

Generating Energy Units (EU)

IC2E's basic generator runs on any item that can fire up a furnace—for example, wood, charcoal, and coal, although lava didn't behave. I prefer charcoal. It's a simple matter to chop down trees, replant the saplings, and place the gathered wood in a furnace to produce charcoal.

Creating your first generator does, however, require quite a few resources, including the crafting of tools such as the forge hammer and cutter that are, fortunately, reused multiple times on the crafting table. In addition, your standard furnace will be working hard smelting away, and you have a moderate amount of mining to do. The generator is made from a machine casing, an RE-Battery, and a cobblestone furnace. Follow these steps, and feel free to pull the resources from the Creative inventory. I'll assume you can look up the recipes using NEI, but I'll list the resources required for each component just so you have an idea of the challenge this poses in Survival mode:

1. Create a forge hammer with five iron ingots and two sticks. This tool can beat ingots into plates 80 times over. It is, in a word, formidable.

2. Place the hammer on the crafting table along with eight iron ingots to form eight iron plates. Place these on the table in the same shape as a furnace to build a basic machine casing. This item is used for most of the machines in IC2E.

The RE-Battery requires insulated tin cable and tin item casing, along with a dash of redstone:

1. Create a cutter with three iron plates this time, the same way as in the preceding steps, and add two iron ingots. Each cutter will last for 60 uses and is needed to make cables.

2. Create three sections of tin cable by combining the cutter with one piece of tin plate. Form the tin plate by combining a tin ingot (smelted from tin ore) with the increasingly well-used hammer.

3. Transform all the cable into insulated tin cable by combining them with three pieces of rubber. You may recall from earlier in this chapter that rubber is smelted from sticky resin. The easiest way to get this is to tap the orange spots on the jungle wood, or use the crossbreeding agricultural method.

4. Create four tin plate pieces by smelting four chunks of tin ore into ingots.

5. Turn the tin plates into tin item casings by beating the plates with the hammer. By this time you're probably feeling ready for the hammer throw event at the next Olympics.

6. Place one piece of insulated tin cable, the four tin item casings, and two pieces of redstone on the crafting table and you'll have yourself an empty RE-Battery.

Finally, build a standard cobblestone furnace and combine it with the machine casing and the RE-Battery. Congratulations, you just bridged the generation gap!

That's a lot of work, requiring in total (including the tools) 18 pieces of iron ore, five tin ore, three sticky resin, and two sticks. Fortunately, tin is very common in the upper levels of the world. You'll find plenty with just a little mining.

But we're not done yet. The generator isn't terribly useful. It can produce power (see Figure 8.16) but has nowhere to put it. You can solve that by making another two batteries. This time, each will only take four tin ingots and another two redstone because you already have two lengths of spare cable.

Charge them up and you'll be able to perform two full sets of scans with the Cropnalyzer.

It's a start, but you'll probably want to consider creating a BatPack next. It takes six of the batteries, an electronic circuit formed from six insulated copper cables, an iron plate, two redstone, and a rather simple block of wood. The BatPack gives you a whopping 60,000 EU on tap wherever you go.

The basic generator also lies at the heart of most of the more advanced types, but you can also tap the energy produced by this one and apply it to many other tasks.

FIGURE 8.16   Place an empty battery into the top slot of a generator, fuel such as charcoal in the lower, and it will get to work. The last two numbers in the tooltip are an estimated countdown in seconds until the charging completes.

Mining, Macerating, and More

Now that you have the power (yes, you do!), it's time to put it to good use. This is not just a battery charger like the type you plug into the wall to juice up your phone. No sir. The following are some of the possibilities.

Automated Mining

The two mining machines in IC2E are quite different from the ones in BuildCraft. The most basic of them will dig a shaft straight down to bedrock, but with the addition of the OD or OV Scanners it can seek out ores in a 5×5 or 9×9 area and only dig out other materials such as cobblestone, gravel, and dirt as it automatically branches out underground driving its drill bit straight toward them (see Figure 8.17). One note: The OD Scanner draws energy away from the mining operation until it's fully charged to 100K EU, and the OV Scanner has to reach 1M EU.

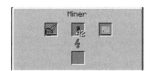

FIGURE 8.17   Mining its own business: This basic miner is primed with pipe, an electric drill, and an OD Scanner to dig out ores in a 5×5 area.

Figure 8.18 shows a sample layout for connecting the generator to the miner. You don't need a fancy cable: just a piece of straight or insulated tin cabling will suffice. You can also place the generator directly adjacent the miner. Put a chest on the other side to pull in the results so they don't get tossed out the top as loose drops. Figure 8.19 shows an extension from that into a BuildCraft sorting system. Use a wooden extraction pipe and redstone engine from BuildCraft to draw the items from the chest. You can use the diamond pipe sorting function to send the gravel, cobblestone, and dirt to a void pipe for destruction, or send them wherever you desire, while all the ores flow straight into the other chest.

FIGURE 8.18 The chest next to the miner catches the results. I've dug out a few blocks in front to show the miner's pipe shaft extending down.

FIGURE 8.19 Although BuildCraft pipes can't connect directly to the miner, they can to its chest.

The basic miner does have one failing: It will stop working the moment it hits water or lava. You can solve this by adding a pump to the back of the miner, connecting it to the power supply and filling it with a few empty universal fluid cells.

Break the miner with a wrench when it's finished, and all the pipe segments get sucked back up into the adjacent chest. Unfortunately, the drill bit stays behind, so there is a slight cost to relocating miners.

The advanced miner requires a huge energy supply to get started, but has several distinct advantages that include having a built-in sorting function, not requiring pipe segments or a drill bit, and providing a coordinate readout that can give you an idea of how far it has to go before hitting bedrock. When it's close, and nothing more flows, it's time to move it on.

Macerators and More

Once you have the basic generator and miner set up, you'll easily be able to quickly add all the ores you need without having to head down into the bowels of the Overworld. Here are a few other machines you can add to the collection as your resources grow:

- **Macerators**—These hungry devices chew ores into two pieces of dust. Smelting that dust in a furnace results in two ingots, where you would previously have received just one. They are relatively cheap to build, and the results will double the output from any mining operation.

- **Extractors**—Get more bang from your organic buck with these multiplying machines. They'll deliver three rubber blocks from one sticky resin, and will similarly transform rubber wood and harvested leaves. They're hard to beat because rubber is one of the most needed elements in IC2E.

- **Compressors**—These tough customers do exactly as their name suggests, squishing base substances into more exotic materials, many of which are required for the more advanced devices. They can even compress coal into diamonds.

All these machines have far more advanced upgrades, but the path toward them is fairly balanced. With just these few machines and a basic generator, you can start on quite a journey, adding more powerful generators that operate off a wide variety of fuel sources, building machines that require the additional power, and having a lot of productive fun along the way.

CAUTION

Overloading Cables and Machines

Although the details are too complicated to go into here, you should be wary of using cables that are too light for the current they need to carry as well as feeding too much power into machines. Both will lead to explosions of a rather drastic nature. You can find an excellent summary of EU as well as the limits of cables and machines at this link: http://tekkitclassic.wikia.com/wiki/EU.

There is one final topic left before we depart this chapter. I hope it doesn't go off with a bang.

Going Thermonuclear

A nuclear reactor delivers more power than you might ever think you can use. It produces more than enough to run the fabulous mass fabricator that is able to produce almost every element in *Minecraft* from a single ingredient. We're going to build a very simple one here for the sake of the exercise. Why not more power? Well, see the cautionary note "The Big Bang, In Theory." In fact, there is so much rework going to this section of IC2E that I can't guarantee the following steps will work by the time you read this book. But if you're up for the challenge, please continue. What's the worst that could happen? (I'm not going to answer that; it would spoil the surprise. Just build this at least 30 blocks away from home.)

CAUTION

The Big Bang, In Theory

A nuclear reactor can deliver more power than you might ever think you can use, and also run the enormously fabulous mass fabricator that can produce almost every element in *Minecraft* out of a single ingredient called UU-Matter. However, in IC2E, at this writing (Build 2.2.598), there is major reconstruction taking place with a complete and rather exciting rework of the entire nuclear system. The IC2E add-on called Nuclear Control is also pending an update waiting on these changes. If you decide to experiment with nuclear power, I highly recommend you don't decide to do so in your basement. It's just not worth the risk should something go wrong.

We're going to build the simplest and safest possible reactor. Do this in Creative mode, following these steps:

1. Remember, safety first: Put on a hazmat suit. You'll be holding uranium ore and definitely don't want to become a medical case study. Hazmat suits are composed of a hazmat suit (the chest plate), hazmat leggings, rubber boots, and a scuba helmet.

2. Once you're all zipped up, place a random block on the ground. Its only purpose is to prop up the central reactor, and will be removed later to make room for an additional reactor chamber.

3. Fetch a nuclear reactor from the inventory, along with nine fuel rods (Uranium) and nine heat vents. (The heat vents conveniently stack if fetched with NEI, but otherwise you'll need to grab them one at a time.) Pick up a redstone lever at the same time.

4. Attach the lever to the side of the temporary block and place the reactor on top. Why the lever? Reactors switch on with a redstone current. Be brave, and flick the lever to turn it on.

5. Now for the fun part, if you weren't having much already. Right-click the reactor to open its window and load in one fuel rod and one heat vent, ensuring they are adjacent to each other, as shown in Figure 18.20. As soon as they're in place, the reactor springs into action, or limps, rather, with 5 EU/t output. Not much, I know, but it is your own personal nuclear reactor.

6. Let's load it up a bit because 5 EU/t is barely enough to get a miner out of bed. Place the remaining fuel rods and heat vents as shown in Figure 8.21. Now you should see 45 EU/t. That's more like it.

7. You may have noticed all those X's in the other slots in the reactor window. They're locked off because the reactor is lacking additional reaction chambers. Grab six reactor chambers (not additional nuclear reactors) from the inventory, knock the block out of the bottom of the original, and attach a chamber to each of its six surfaces. Reattach the lever to the outside of one of the new chambers. You'll end up with a rather ominous pile of potential nuclear meltdown looking like Figure 8.22.

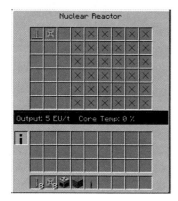

FIGURE 8.20 Low power output but, hey, how many people have one of these?

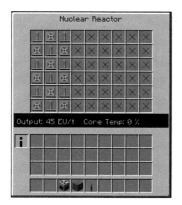

FIGURE 8.21 Turning up the dial, although only to nine.

FIGURE 8.22 Creating a full-size nuclear reactor, without a sign of a protest group.

8. Right-click any of the chambers and you'll see the full reactor's inventory. Repeat the pattern across the board with another 27 fuel rods and heat vents (see Figure 8.23). Congratulations, you now have a reactor outputting 135 EU/t. Remember, with great power comes great responsibility. Use it wisely.

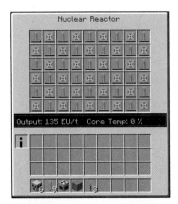

FIGURE 8.23 Although this is at best an inefficient, low-production reactor layout, it shouldn't blow up—fingers crossed.

The Bottom Line

One of the interesting things about the design of IC2E is not so much that it adds a host of new machines and so on—although that *is* spectacular—but rather that the mod makers took one of the somewhat humdrum activities from the vanilla game and made it so much more useful. I am, of course, talking about farming.

Players only need so much virtual food to keep the health bar propped up, and the relatively small automated farms described in Chapter 2, "Automated Produce Farms," more than suffice. But what if farms could produce more? What if there were plants that turned into iron and gold? Now we have a good reason to begin the pursuit.

I haven't discovered a good way yet to fully automate IC2E farms. The planting of the crop stakes is the problem. But perhaps there'll be a way once BuildCraft implements its flying robots.

The interesting balance between crossbreeding, aiming for the best attributes, and fighting off weed infestations adds numerous dynamics to what could have been a rather ordinary process.

The new electrical tools and weapons (hello, NanoSaber) are also a lot of fun. Strap on a jetpack and descend on mobs from above like an avenging angel.

One of the things I couldn't get to in this chapter due to space constraints was the entire recycling of materials into scrap and their subsequent use to also power generators and become part of a chain of production. There are even biogas generators in here. It's an entire framework that could provide a fascinating environmental lesson for kids. Even the spent fuel from nuclear reactors can be recycled, but do remember to always suit up for the occasion (see Figure 8.24).

IndustrialCraft changed *Minecraft* in many important ways. Then IndustrialCraft² doubled or, perhaps, squared its impact. IndustrialCraft² Experimental is a powerful, imaginative reworking of the core concepts, and early indications are that it is going to do very well indeed.

See you in the next chapter, where we'll go riding on rails.

FIGURE 8.24 Go nuclear, be happy, but don't forget your hazmat suit.

Rolling with Railcraft

In This Chapter

- Create creosote.
- Rail tie it all together.
- Train on tracks.
- Tunnel, bore, and chomp gravel.
- Use mods to expand.

Minecraft's rails system is functional but frustrating. With no way to truly link carts together, and difficulty in setting up track junctions, it's not so much the age of the iron horse as it is a wooden donkey.

Enter Railcraft, a complete reimagining of the minecart system. Railcraft brings with it the following key additions:

- Cart linking that works. Admittedly, *Minecraft* has never promised this, but the linking is so much more effective than trying to push carts ahead.
- Numerous additional cart types, including those that can transport energy and liquids and even keep their section of the world loaded and running when you're not nearby. This is perfect for automated farms or sending carts between distant places.
- A new fuel source—yep, we're getting steamy.
- High-speed tracks and many other types of tracks, including those that are one way, reducing the risk of a collision.
- A signaling system and all kinds of control parameters.
- And, my favorite, the tunnel bore (see Figure 9.1).

Railcraft also brings with it a complete reworking of track construction, and it takes quite a bit of work to get going.

As with BuildCraft and IndustrialCraft, Railcraft is a massive mod, so this chapter will act as an introduction. Interestingly, it also works rather perfectly with both those mods. For example, you can use Buildcraft pipes to shift steam and fluids around, automatically refuel, and so on.

Download Railcraft from here and install in the usual way:

> http://www.railcraft.info/releases/

FIGURE 9.1   The tunnel bore automates the laying of tracks, including laying bridges if necessary, as shown here, and carves out a 3X3 tunnel—more than enough room to run carts.

Getting Started

A certain amount of work is required to get started with Railcraft in Survival mode. The first step is to build a coke oven (not for the fizzy stuff). Historically, coke replaced the use of pure charcoal for smelting and cooking. The coke oven converts coal into coal coke, a fuel source that burns twice as long. It also produces creosote oil as a byproduct, and this is required for crafting wooden tracks.

Follow these steps to create your own and start cranking out creosote:

1. Head to a swamp or river biome with shovel in hand to gather 104 clay and 130 sand. Clay typically exists in the shallow waters, with each block delivering four pieces of clay. Collect a lot of extra sand to smelt into glass and then craft into glass bottles. You'll need this for collecting creosote. Also fetch a stack of wood.

2. Use a furnace to smelt the clay into clay bricks.

3. Craft 36 coke oven bricks using bricks and sand.

4. The coke oven is a 3×3×3 block of bricks with a hollow center. Lay down a 3×3 platform first, then place a ring of eight more bricks on top of that, leaving out the one in the middle (see Figure 9.2).

5. Cap it with a 3×3 roof of the same bricks. As soon as you place the final block on top the structure will convert to a single large item as shown in Figure 9.3.

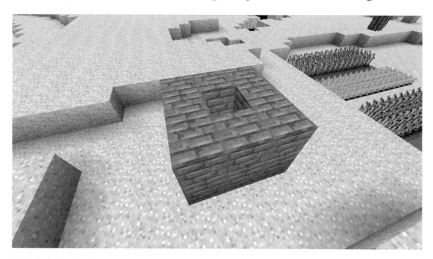

FIGURE 9.2 Creating a coke oven.

FIGURE 9.3 Creating a coke oven.

6. Right-click the oven and place coal in the leftmost slot. Gather the coal coke from the middle slot.

5. Creosote gradually builds up in the tank in the middle. Gather it by placing empty glass bottles in the top-right slot. They'll fill automatically and drop down into the bottom-right slot as shown in Figure 9.4. It's a slow process: Each piece of coal takes around three minutes to convert to coal coke, along with producing a small quantity of creosote oil. If you have the resources, feel free to build a second or even third oven to speed things up.

FIGURE 9.4   Creating creosote is the first step in building wooden rails.

There are more steps to creating rails in Railcraft, but the resources are similar—it just takes a bit more time.

Rather than making rails from a single recipe, you'll need to take a few steps:

1. Craft wooden rail ties at the standard crafting table. They're expensive as you'll need three plank slabs and a bottle of creosote for each. Gather the filled creosote bottles and start making the ties using the creosote and the slabs. Make as many as you can.

2. Create wooden rails using an iron ingot and one wooden rail tie. Each produces six rails.

3. Combine four rail ties into a wooden rail bed.

4. Craft six rails and one wooden rail bed to produce 32 segments of wooden track.

Wooden track is the least effective of the tracks in Railcraft. It's slow and steady, but won't win any races. The standard track steps things up, but requires a few additional steps as it needs iron rails.

Creating Standard Track

The method for making standard *Minecraft* tracks varies with the Railcraft mod.

Iron rails are created at a rolling machine formed from four steel ingots, four pistons, and a crafting table. Power a rolling machine with a steam engine from Railcraft or a sterling engine or better from Buildcraft. Regular redstone engines don't deliver sufficient power.

Figure 9.5 shows a fairly standard setup. The rails are sent to the chest automatically, although it's possible to also send them elsewhere with BuildCraft pipes.

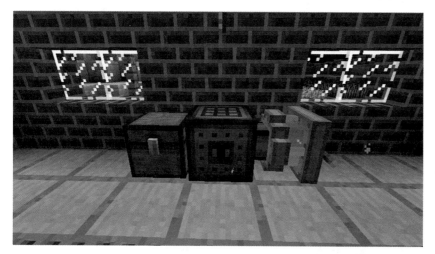

FIGURE 9.5 Rolling machine, steam engine, and chest.

By the way, Railcraft kindly adds train stations to villages. Inside the station you'll find the configuration shown in Figure 9.5. Add coal to the steam engine to fire it up. You can see the standard station in Figure 9.6. It's a great way to get started faster in a survival game.

FIGURE 9.6 The default station added by Buildcraft during world generation.

Follow these steps to start making tracks:

1. Fire up the steam engine by giving it a fuel source, as shown in Figure 9.7, and add water. (Keep the water topped up with Buildcraft pipes if necessary. Filling an empty but hot steam engine may cause major trauma in the form of an explosion.)

2. Feed iron ingots into the rolling machine to produce rails (see Figure 9.8).

3. Combine them at a crafting table with the wooden rail bed to produce standard track.

Although these steps are significant, you get a lot of track for your buck, 32 pieces in all, so in the long run it's actually slightly cheaper on resources to build rails this way, and you can keep the rolling machine fed with Buildcraft pipes so that it continues automatically. Give it a higher supply of energy (it can consume up to 5 MJ/t) to run a little faster.

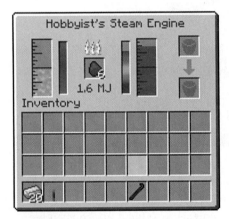

FIGURE 9.7 Steam engines use water and fuel. Switch them on with a redstone signal or lever.

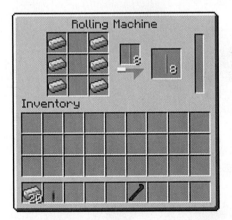

FIGURE 9.8 Making rails with the rolling machine.

Wooden and standard track are just the beginning. Consider crafting and using these additional types of rails:

- **Locking track**—Halt that train! Feed these rails some redstone current and they will act like the standard powered rail, but when unpowered they seize any cart passing over the top to prevent it moving. Why? Well, mobs can't move the cart, and this makes it wonderfully useful for designing stations.

- **Embarking tracks**—These neat parallels whip you into the cart automatically, whether you're ready or not—perfect for that Adventure mode experience, or just surprising the heck out of someone.

- **Launch track**—Major Tom? Give this track some redstone power and it will fling any cart passing over the top to interesting heights. You can change the launch force by right-clicking with the crowbar (see the "Always Carry a Crowbar" tip).

TIP

Always Carry a Crowbar

Crowbars are an essential tool for all Railcraft engineers. Keep one in your pocket at all times. Like the Buildcraft wrench, a crowbar changes the direction of some Railcraft blocks such as the cart dispenser. You can also use them to easily rip up old track, to change the direction of a locomotive's travel, and, most importantly, to link carts together. Ensure the carts are no more than two blocks apart, then shift right-click each cart to form a bond. Create a crowbar from four pieces of red dye and three iron ingots.

- **Coupler track**—Actually, one of a pair. These tracks can link (or delink with the decoupler) carts as they pass over the top.

- **Elevator tracks**—Climb cliffs with alacrity. Ascend great heights (see Figure 9.9). Elevator tracks are like a ladder for minecarts. When powered, the elevator tracks can transport your carts up vertical cliff faces; unpowered, they allow for a gentle descent back down. Create a transition to the elevator track by placing your normal track on the horizontal surface up to the edge of the ascent, then place the elevator track two blocks above. This lifts the normal track up to the start of the elevator track. Run normal track directly to the elevator track at the top of the ascent. It will make a 90 degree corner, but minecarts run over that quite smoothly.

FIGURE 9.9 Get a quick lift with elevator tracks, but keep in mind that they don't work with linked carts.

- **High-speed track**—High-speed tracks are 2.5 times faster than normal tracks, but come with certain risks. Turns must be carefully managed by slowing the cart to normal speeds with an unpowered high-speed booster track or by zipping down the transition track. On the other hand, this track may well be the fastest way to move around *Minecraft* unless you are flying in Spectator mode.

- **Junctions**—Yes, finally you can cross over with ease. Junction tracks form a four-way intersection and allow the tracks to cross without becoming infernally confused. Railcraft also has a wye ("Y") junction to handle three-way intersections at increased speeds, and an improved switching track with a visual indicator.

Reinforced Tracks

It won't take you long to want to move beyond the basics of wooden and standard tracks. While these tracks provide improvements on the standard *Minecraft* fare, including a speed-limiting characteristic that will prevent your character from becoming mincemeat on a turn—steel yourself: Reinforced track is 25% faster than the normal and blast resistant, so it can shrug off hostile mobs, or even an irate ghast from the Nether, with ease.

Follow these steps to create a better track than the standard rail:

1. Create steel with a blast furnace (see Figure 9.10). This will take some building. This furnace is built the same way as a coke oven, except there are two hollow layers in the middle instead of one, and the 34 blast furnace bricks require more exotic ingredients. You'll need to head to The Nether to collect Netherbrick, soul sand, and magma cream.

2. Load the furnace with coal coke (you can even do this automatically with Buildcraft pipes straight from the coke oven) and then feed it a steady supply of iron ingots to convert them into steel.

FIGURE 9.10   Blast furnaces convert iron to steel and are one block higher than a coke oven.

3. While the furnace is burning away, make rebar in the rolling machine using three iron ingots laid out diagonally from bottom left to upper right.

4. Combine one rebar with three stone slabs to form stone ties. As with the wooden rails, make as many of these as you can.

5. Use four stone ties to create a stone railbed.

6. Use the rolling machine to convert the steel and obsidian dust into reinforced rail.

7. Combine six rails with the stone rail bed at the crafting table to create 32 segments of reinforced track.

Reinforced track takes a lot of work, but it's almost indestructible nature makes it well worthwhile.

Now let's move on to something a little more fun: tunnel boring. Yes, once you start, you'll never want to stop.

Boring, Not So

Sick of digging ditches? Want to throw the shovel into the nearest pile of dirt? The tunnel borer is Railcraft's patent-pending solution to tossing dirt and gravel over your shoulder (see Figure 9.11).

Feed it fuel (or anything you might burn in a furnace), gravel, tracks, and a bore head, and it will take off into the distance.

FIGURE 9.11   Using the tunnel borer to dig out long tunnels is a hands off exercise in ore discovery.

The borer digs a 3×3 hole while laying down tracks. It's smart enough to backfill any depressions with gravel to ensure an even rail bed, but will also pause when hitting flowing water at its own level, lava, or a hole deeper than 10 blocks.

The main usable component is the bore head itself. You can create one from iron (digging for around 160 blocks), steel (around 320 blocks), or diamond (tunneling almost 700 blocks). Only a diamond head can dig obsidian, but chances are you'll use this machine higher than the obsidian levels.

Here are some tips for the successful use of your borer:

- Link chest carts to the tunnel bore to provide it with additional supplies when the bore itself starts to run low.

- Linked chest carts also collect the blocks removed by the borer so they don't litter the landscape. Well, they should. There's a bug in the current version that will hopefully be fixed by the time you read this.

- Connect an anchor cart to ensure the borer keeps boring even if your player's character is not near.

The tunnel bore can save you from extreme tedium but it also exposes a lot of ores. Follow in its footsteps to discover a trove of valuable items.

Creating a tunnel bore is not easy. You need to craft it from two furnaces, a couple of blocks of steel, two minecarts, and a minecart with chest. Then there's the borehead. An iron head has the same mining limitations as an iron pickaxe and doesn't last very long. It can dig a tunnel 160 blocks long. Steel from the blast furnace is much stronger, managing 320 blocks. Diamond takes the cake being able to dig a tunnel 700 blocks long.

Link a chest cart to the bore to collect dropped items. Link an anchor cart to ensure the bore keeps working even if you are not nearby. Figure 9.12 shows an example.

FIGURE 9.12 Link a chest and a minecart with a hopper to the borer to collect drops. Add an anchor cart to keep it operating even when you're not present.

The tunnel bore is somewhat unique in its configuration. Right-click it to open the window shown in Figure 9.13. It needs feeding. A bore head, fuel to run, ballast to fill in those gaps in the ground, and track to lay as it moves forward.

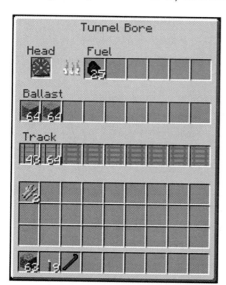

FIGURE 9.13 Give a tunnel bore what it needs and it will do the rest, diligently digging its tunnel, laying track, filling in ground, and, in all ways, carving a path.

Undercutting the Competition

Tracks on natural terrain look, well, like tracks on natural terrain. If you want your railbed to have a more industrial look, consider the undercutter. It scoots over the top, replacing the blocks beneath each track segment. You could replace the blocks with gravel (predictable) or go for crushed obsidian. How do you get that? With a stone crusher.

By the way, don't forget the associated track relayer. It can tear up your slow-mo wooden track and replace it with one that's reinforced, or high speed. Linking an undercutter to a relayer and then attaching them to a rail engine will give you a two-step replacement system that can upgrade all your rails and the underlying railbeds.

> **TIP**
>
> **Item Loaders, Part Deux**
>
> Item loaders solve all the problems hoppers present. They'll keep a cart underneath until it's full, then fire off a redstone signal to send it on its way. Deliver the loader's signal to a boarding track to make it work seamlessly.

More Mods

Part of the delight of *Minecraft* is its seemingly never-ending collection of mods made by other inspired creators. The list is fabulous, inventive, and entertaining.

Before we end this guide, I want to share some of my favorites with you. This by no means takes into account the full panoply; rather, these are the more significant ones that add interesting goals to the game.

Indeed, it should probably be said that these mods add so many more goals to the game. They expand it, extend, embrace in a balanced way, and build to the point that each would be a worthy contender for a complete game on its own. I remain in awe of their authors.

Galacticraft

Reach for the stars. Galacticraft adds planets, spacecraft, and the attendant prerequisites of oxygen management to *Minecraft*. Fly to the moon or colonize Mars. You'll have an interesting time due to resource restrictions, but also enjoy gamboling in lower gravity.

Building a rocket isn't easy, but oh so worthwhile. You'll need to refine oil into rocket fuel, compress oxygen into tanks, and create a parachute, a launch pad and... oh yes, the rocket itself.

Once you reach the moon, there are new villagers to meet, and you can do a little bit of terraforming by planting trees and gathering the oxygen. You'll also need a sealable base and so much more. Read more at http://goo.gl/VZX8RN.

Forestry

The bees are in trouble. Fancy helping out with a spot of apiary? What about adding a complete agrarian spin to *Minecraft*? The forestry mod has become an agricultural tour de force.

Besides the bees, the forestry plug-in adds automated farms (feed-in water, fertilizer, soil, and seeds) and will deliver harvested resources and waste into a connected inventory or Buildcraft transport pipe.

ComputerCraft

It makes sense in a way to bring programming in-game to *Minecraft*. And not just any language—the ComputerCraft mod adds programmable turtles to the game. The name *turtle* harkens back to turtle graphics, a beginner's programming language that would send a cursor around the screen. However—and as a programmer I find this very cool—ComputerCraft's LUA language does it in the *Minecraft* environment, so it becomes 3D. The LUA language, which originated in a university in Brazil, is also far more capable and has become the leading scripting engine in computer games—and not just lightweights: We're looking at *World of Warcraft*, *Lego MindStorms*, and many others.

If a degree in IT is desired for a young one, nothing can beat that which delivers immediate results. LUA within *Minecraft* does just this. Create a few lines of code and see what happens. There's nothing that comes close.

The Bottom Line

Writing a more advanced guide to *Minecraft* has been a journey in itself. *Minecraft* has turned into an ecosystem supporting hundreds of people, some of whom have become the highest earning contributors on YouTube. They have become legend through mod packs and music videos (well, the parodies—if you haven't seen them, just search for "Minecraft Video Parodies").

The incredible creative energy poured into this endeavor is beyond any I've seen. *Minecraft*, although a fascinating and very complete game on its own terms, has become a blank canvas upon which so much more can be written.

Perhaps the most exciting part of this is that *Minecraft* v1.8 is due in just a few days as of this writing (Fall 2014). It's the biggest update in the game's history, and brings with it numerous improvements.

To add to a somewhat salacious part of the debate about v1.8, the modding API will allow much better compatibility for mods of all kinds, but I expect Forge will continue to be a part of the system. It is more likely Forge will see an update for 1.8, and all the current major mods will continue to use the Forge APIs rather than switching to a new system.

In any case, loaders such as MultiMC and the amazing mod packs put together by others such as Direwolf20, Yogscraft, dan200, sirsengir, and more, will continue to build on a base experience that has become infinitely more.

Enjoy all *Minecraft* has to offer. Start a new world. Use the mods detailed herein on Survival. It's an experience that continues to grow, develop, and reward.

Recording and Sharing

In This Chapter

- Choose the right software.
- Plot camera paths and animation.
- Overlay audio and titles.
- Publish to YouTube, Vimeo, or in HD.

With its soaring constructions, ingenious mob traps, and rollercoaster mine rides, *Minecraft* really lends itself to sharing knowledge and adventures through video (see Figure 10.1). By now, I'm sure you've wondered how you to show off your own hard work and creativity by publishing your world online. In this chapter, I will take you through the process of choosing the right capturing and editing software, picking functionality and use, adding titles and music, and, finally, uploading your masterpiece onto the Web to share with the world!

FIGURE 10.1 Get ready to show your creations to the world. Lights, camera, action!

Choosing the Right Software

Many solutions are available for recording video for both PC and Mac users, with varied cost and features.

To get started, you first need to decide which screen-recording method you wish to use. You have two options, and each has its benefits and drawbacks:

- **Software recording**—An application (via online download or disc) that records whatever is onscreen while you play *Minecraft*.
  - **Benefits:** This is the most cost-effective method because no additional hardware is required.
  - **Drawbacks:** Depending on your computer's processor speed, current load, and graphics card specifications, you may experience frame lag and "jumpy" video captures.
- **Hardware recording**—An external piece of hardware, separate from your computer, that plugs in between your graphics card and monitor and records everything displayed on your screen. Video is captured to an external storage device (such as an SD card, CompactFlash card, or USB disk) or the computer's internal hard drive.
  - **Benefits:** The capture and real-time image compression is done by the device, thus reducing the load on the computer. Because of this, you can consistently capture at a very high frame rate regardless of the load your PC is under at the time. This produces a smooth video result.
  - **Drawbacks:** Generally, this solution costs more than the software solution because you'll require additional hardware and associated leads.

> **NOTE**
>
> **The More Constant the Frame Rate, the Smoother the Video**
>
> Frame rate is the number of single frames per second at which a moving video animation is being generated or captured. The majority of videos you see on TV, online, and on your mobile device are rendered between 24fps and 30fps (frames per second). When you're capturing a video, the frame rate needs to be at least 25fps, but more importantly, the frame rate needs to be constant. A slower, less powerful computer may struggle to capture at a higher frame rate consistently, which could result in "jumpy" video. Most screen-recording tools will allow you to specify the frame rate, so it's best to experiment with what works best for your setup. *Minecraft* renders at 60fps on the PC by default, but be mindful that your final video will be converted to the default 25–30fps when edited and published online.

All screen-recording tools, using either method, work in pretty much the same way. They allow you to capture video of a full screen, or the contents of a specific window, to a video file. Some tools will also capture live audio (both audio produced from *Minecraft* as well as from a microphone). Let's take a look at the key ones.

FRAPS for Windows (License Approximately $40)

The FRAPS software can be downloaded at http://www.fraps.com, with a free trial offered. (The title is a short version of "FRAmes Per Second.") This software is simple to use. Just download the FRAPS installer and run it using the default settings. Recommended settings are shown in Figure 10.2, including the frame rate and folder to capture video to. If you'd like to record audio from the game, ensure the **Record sound** check box is selected.

Once FRAPS is running, load *Minecraft* as you would normally. You will notice a green number at the top left of your screen. This will not be displayed in your video, but is there to indicate that FRAPS is monitoring the screen and displaying the current FPS.

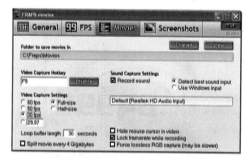

FIGURE 10.2 Configuring FRAPS. Click the **Movies** tab and use default settings.

When you're ready to begin recording, push the F9 key, which will change the indicator digits to red. The number should remain at a constant fps. You can move around in *Minecraft* as you normally do while FRAPS records your screen. Easy!

To finish recording, push the F9 key again. You can repeat this process multiple times, and the captured video files will be stored in your designated folder, as individual AVI files. Depending on your screen resolution while recording, these files could be quite large, so make sure you have spare disk space. Once you edit the files, they'll be converted to a smaller file size, so they can be uploaded. Note that the trial version will only record 30 seconds of video at a time and adds a watermark to the results.

You can preview the captured files with Windows Media Player and check the quality of the video. Make sure you close FRAPS before watching the videos because FRAPS will diligently add the fps to the top of your video in Media Player!

Bandicam for Windows (License Approx. $39)

Bandicam can be downloaded at www.bandicam.com, with a free trial that provides a 10 min recording limit and also adds a watermark to the video.

This is a great tool that works very similarly to FRAPS. Bandicam has a few extra benefits. It produces videos in a variety of formats and resolutions, so you can experiment and find the best setup to suit your needs. Running with the default settings produces great results, and the software is preconfigured to record game audio.

Recording is easy. Load *Minecraft* in one window, then load Bandicam in a second window. Within Bandicam is a button that looks like a game controller. Click this button and then click the *Minecraft* window. This action tells Bandicam which window you wish to capture from.

The green fps numbers should appear at the top left of the *Minecraft* window. Once you are ready to record, simply push the F12 key to begin capturing video (see Figure 10.3). When you have finished, push F12 to stop. You can view the captured videos by selecting the **Output** tab on the left, and they will appear in a list. Double-click to select and view one.

FIGURE 10.3 Click the game controller button, then the Minecraft window. Push F12 to start recording.

QuickTime Player for Mac (Free with OS X)

This feature is a bonus from the staple Apple application QuickTime. It's very easy to use, and there's no additional cost. Simply run QuickTime Player and then choose **File, New Screen Recording**. You can choose one of two options: perform a full screen capture or just capture a selected region on your screen.

For the latter, simply drag a window selection (see Figure 10.4) over your *Minecraft* window. You will be prompted to begin recording. If you would like to run *Minecraft* in full screen, choose the full screen option or just select the *Minecraft* window to capture its contents.

The completed file will be an Apple QuickTime .mov file, which is a very common format that's supported by most platforms.

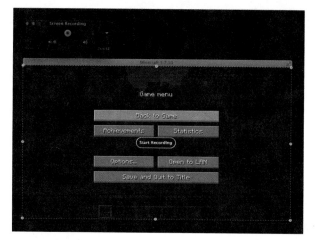

FIGURE 10.4 Drag a selection region over your *Minecraft* window and QuickTime will begin recording.

NOTE

Recording Resolution

Something important to consider while using any of the recording tools is the resolution of your captured video. With FRAPS and Bandicam, for example, the size of your *Minecraft* window will define the dimensions of the video file that is captured. If you run Minecraft in full screen, this will maximize the resolution of the captured video, but will also affect the frame rate. This is where the fps counter comes in handy. As previously mentioned, you need to keep the frame rate at or above 25fps. A bit of experimentation may be required to find your optimum window size in order to maintain a constant frame rate. Try to find a balance between gaining the highest resolution possible without sacrificing your frame rate, and vice versa.

TIP

Lighten the Load

To ensure the highest capture quality on a Windows PC, it is always best to close any programs and windows you are not using at the time of capturing your video. Because recording is very resource intensive, you need to ensure your computer has as much CPU and memory capacity available as possible. If you have a large image desktop background, or a fancy theme in Windows, it is worthwhile changing it to something plain and basic while you record. This simple action will have a large impact on your video quality.

Hardware Recording Devices

The following hardware devices are designed to plug in to your computer's display card and record the output as it is displayed on your monitor. This method of recording is particularly useful if you wish to make full-screen, high-definition (HD) -recordings at a high frame rate. The result is a very high-quality video, suitable for professional-level video captures. Of course, this standard of quality does come at a price, but is not as expensive as you might expect.

I've tested two devices listed next with excellent results. Both are compatible with Windows and OS X.

AVerMedia's Live Gamer Portable (RRP $169)

This device records the HD video and audio output of any HDMI source directly to your PC via USB, or onto an SD card which you can then load into your computer for editing. The latter function means you don't have to have a PC connected when recording the video, which means it is also very handy for recording independent gaming consoles and non-networked devices.

The LGP is very easy to use, simply push the button on the top of the device to start and stop recording.

Elgato Game Capture HD Recorder (RRP $199)

Similarly to the AVerMedia device, Elgato connects to the HDMI output of your PC or game console and records full HD video using high-speed hardware video compression. Recording software is included with the hardware. The device plugs in to your PC and then uses the computer hard drive to store captured video. Although this is similar to using a software-recording tool such as FRAPS or Bandicam, it does have one major advantage: All the hard work of capture and compression is being completed by the Elgato, so your computer can dedicate its resources to render *Minecraft* in the highest frame rate.

Plotting Camera Paths and Animation

So, you've now learned how to capture video, but perhaps would like your masterpiece to be a little more exciting than Minecraft Steve tending his crops. You may have seen online videos in which the camera seems attached to an aircraft flying heroically through the world, boasting panning views and changing camera angles. Let's now look at the best ways to show off your world before we capture it to video.

You'll need one or more mods to film aerial video. The key one for capturing the video is Camera Studio mod, available on the Minecraft Forum at http://goo.gl/dfLVJe.

You'll also want to fly for those great aerial shots. In creative mode, I'm sure you have flown many times by double-tapping the spacebar and using Shift to descend. In survival mode, however, you don't have this benefit. To use the Camera Studio mod, you need the virtual ability to take your "camera" to the specific positions from which you wish to shoot. In other words, gravity is not your friend.

A few modpacks are available (such as XRay and Zombe) that allow you to fly in survival mode. The mods use different action keys than you would use when flying in creative mode, but with the same result.

Now that you have donned your spandex and super cape, you can begin planning out your video. If you've done any video editing or animation before, you will already be familiar with the concept of keyframes. In case not, let's have a quick look at it now.

Keyframes are points within an animation or sequence where you can set properties of the camera or objects. The keyframes always exist in order on a timeline. With your Camera Studio mod, you are able to move the camera using your normal player movement controls and set multiple keyframes that the camera will follow when you begin recording (see Figure 10.5).

FIGURE 10.5 Move your camera to various positions within your world, each time selecting P to set a new camera point.

For example, let's pretend we are filming a virtual tour of your Minecraft village. You want to finish by entering a house for a tour of its features.

To do this, move your camera to each of the different places you wish to capture, and record a keyframe (press the P key) at each individual position. Using a Hansel and Gretel analogy, this is like leaving breadcrumbs for the camera to follow. The mod will take note of the position of the camera at each place and the direction it was pointing. You are also able to change the roll/angle of the camera at each point, to add another dimension to your flying footage.

Once all your keyframes are set, you can watch the camera moving through them chronologically by typing **/cam start**.

A full list of controls and shortcuts can be viewed or modified by hitting the O key (see Figure 10.6). Some of the shortcuts I commonly use are listed next (you may need to add the shortcut keys through the options screen yourself):

- **P**—This records the keyframe of your current position. Each time you press this key, a new keyframe is added to the list. It can also be set by typing **/cam p**.

- **.**—This starts and stops the "playback" of the camera moving through the keyframes (equivalent to **/cam start /cam stop**).

- **K**—Rolls the camera to the left.

- **L**—Rolls the camera to the right.

- **,**—Brings the roll of the camera back to center.

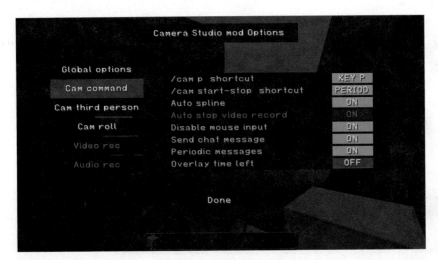

FIGURE 10.6 Hit O to view and edit your shortcut keys and other configuration settings for the Camera Studio mod.

Here are a few other useful commands:

- **/cam start 20s (your desired length of sequence, in seconds)**—The lower the number, the faster the camera will move through the sequence.

- **/cam clear**—This clears all your keyframes.

- **/cam save {any name you like}**—Saves the full sequence of camera keyframes.

- **/cam load {name of previous sequence you saved}**—Loads a previously saved sequence.

- **/cam list**—Lists all the settings saved so far.

You can do many cool things with this mod, and the full command set can be found online. However, one of my favorites is the ability to make the camera focus on a particular point while it moves through each of your keyframes.

Say you have already set up 10 keyframes for your camera. It starts off in the distance and then flies up to a village and then flies a circle around the village. Do you want the camera to be looking at a tower in the center of the village while it circles around it? Easy! After you have set your keyframes, just move your camera to the tower and simply type /**cam target**. This will then ensure the camera always keeps the targeted position (in this case, the center of your village) in the crosshairs while it follows the keyframe circuit.

Recording Using Camera Studio

The detailed instructions for using Camera Studio can be found on the Camera Studio mod download page, but it is definitely worth checking out the ability to record video directly from *Minecraft* using a new feature of the Camera Studio mod. This allows you to produce high-quality videos and time lapses of your preset camera points. This can be very useful if you want to produce smooth and high-quality walkthroughs, flybys, and tours, or show a build in a time-lapse format as you work on it's construction. The screen-recording tools explained earlier in this chapter are more suited for real-time *Minecraft* gameplay.

Overlaying Audio and Titles

In this section I'll guide you through the process of adding audio and titles to your captured video clips. The process is similar across most editing software, but here I'll cover both Windows and OS X use.

First of all, you'll gather together the video clips you have recorded using the methods previously mentioned in this chapter. If you want to add music or other audio to your final video, you'll need to have a copy of the audio files handy. Lastly, you'll need to decide what titles you'd like to use.

Editing with iMovie—OS X (RRP $18.99)

The iMovie software is available for download from the App Store (just type iMovie into the store's search box and it will pop right up).

The first step is to create a new movie by clicking **File, New Movie**. iMovie has lots of great themes you can use to add color and individuality to your video. Once you've chosen your theme, you will be set up with an empty project.

You will notice in Figure 10.7 that four main panes make up the iMovie interface:

- The pane on the far left contains all your libraries. This includes the folders containing your video clips, audio files, and titles.
- The top-left pane contains all the clips for the current project.

- The top-right pane is the video preview window. You can view your video at any point using this interface.

- Lastly, we have the timeline, which contains all the chosen clips that will make up your video. You will notice a vertical line, which is your playhead. You can shift this to any point of the video by holding the handle at the top of the line.

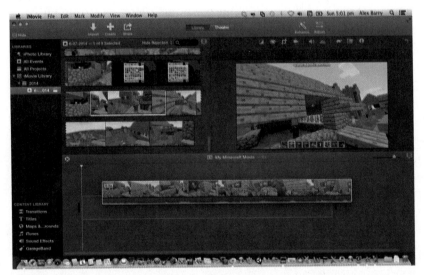

FIGURE 10.7 Drag and drop clips from your library into the timeline in the bottom pane. Change the length of your clips using the handles at each end of the clip.

To get started, drop all your recorded video clips into the top-left pane. You can add as many clips as you need.

You can drag an entire clip onto your timeline, or you can drag your mouse cursor across only the specific section of the clip you wish to use. You will notice an orange box appears that shows the start and end points of the clip that you have selected. To add this section to your video, drag the yellow box down onto the timeline. Only the selected section of the clip will be included. Repeat this process until you have a collection of all the clips you wish to use for the video.

You can change the order of the clips easily by picking them up and moving backward and forward in the timeline. You can also tweak the start and end points of each clip by picking up the handles at the beginning and end of it.

Titles

Once you have your clips in the order you want and are happy with the video, you can start adding titles. Apple have made this process easy. By simply selecting **Titles** in the left library pane, you can generate a list of many different animated titles in the top-left pane. You can preview these by mousing over them.

To include a title in your clip, just drag and drop the selected title style into your timeline, preferably in the section the title will appear. You will see a new title clip has been created in the timeline. You will also notice the words "Title text here" appear in your video preview window in the top-right pane. To edit the title, double-click the text and type in whatever you like.

Note that you can drag the title to a space in between clips, and a title with a black background will be created. Alternatively, drag the title above one of your video clips in the timeline to place the title directly over the top, which is very useful. You have to hand it to Apple—they know how to write user-friendly software!

Adding Audio to Your Movie

Adding audio is a simple affair. You can drag an audio file into the same top-left pane that you dragged your video files into. You will notice that your iTunes library is in the left pane, giving you convenient access to all your stored music (see Figure 10.8). Once you have located the audio file you want to use, simply drag it into the timeline. Underneath the video clip section is a music note icon—drag it here and you can't go wrong. Again, you are able to change the start and end points of your audio file by dragging the handles at either end of the clip.

FIGURE 10.8 It's all about dragging and dropping items onto your timeline. Add titles and audio to your movie, quickly and easily.

Exporting Your Completed Movie

Once you've finished your video, you need to export it, ready to upload to the Web. Simply click **File, Share** and then choose the option that suits you. iMovie allows you to publish your video directly to YouTube, Vimeo, and other social media, but if you wish to manually upload the movie yourself, as explained later in this chapter, then select **File** under **Share**, and you will be prompted to create a movie file. Choose **720p** as the resolution to ensure your video is the highest quality possible.

Editing with Windows Movie Maker—Windows (Free Download)

The Windows Movie Maker software can be downloaded for free at **http://windows. microsoft.com/en-au/windows-live/movie-maker** (http://goo.gl/iIggDb).

The first step is to create a new project by clicking **File, New Project**. You will see two main sections. To the left is a video preview screen. On the right is a clip box labeled **Click here to browse photos or videos**. Click this button and browse to find your recorded clips. You can select multiple files at the same time. Once selected, the clips will be listed in this area, although it may take a few minutes for the software to prepare the files. Once complete, you can see thumbnails for all your recorded clips. Drag the clips into the order you would like them displayed in your video.

Next, you can set the start and end points of each clip. This can be done by moving the playhead (the vertical line at the beginning of the clip) to the point you wish the clip to start. If you right-click **Set Start Point**, this will set the clip to start at that specific point. Use the same method to set the end point for that clip, then move on to the next clip. If you repeat this process for all your clips, you should produce a set of clips that flow well and have no unwanted footage.

Titling

You may wish to add an introductory title to your video. Movie Maker has a lot of fancy options for titles that you should experiment with, but to start, just move the playhead to the beginning of the clip you wish to insert a title before and then click **Title** under the **Home** tab (see Figure 10.9). This will insert a blank title before the selected clip.

Under the new title clip should be a pink bar labeled **My Movie**. If you double-click this, you can edit it to read whatever you like. This change will reflect in the title on your video. By default the title will show on a black background, but you can actually drag the pink bar over one of your recorded clips if you prefer the title displayed over your video footage.

FIGURE 10.9   Once you've dragged your clips into the right pane, all the other tools you need to add titles and audio can be found under the Home tab.

Adding Audio to Your Video

If you'd like to add music to your video, just click **Add music** under the **Home** tab—you can then choose an audio file and specify where the music is to begin. You can set the start and end points for your audio clips in the same way that you do for video clips.

Movie Maker also has the ability to record a narration for the video, which is quite handy. If you wish to record a voiceover, simply click **Record Narration** under the **Home** menu. The video will be played and any audio present via microphone or headset will be recorded.

Exporting Your Completed Video

Once you've finished your video, you need to export it, ready for upload to the Web. Click **File, Save Movie** and then choose the option that suits you.

Movie Maker also allows you to publish your video directly to YouTube, Vimeo and other social media by clicking **File, Publish movie**. Select **Save movie** if you want to manually upload the movie yourself (discussed later in this chapter). Choose your target platform (such as YouTube or Vimeo), and your video will automatically be exported in the correct format, ready to upload.

Publishing to YouTube and Vimeo

Uploading your final video is quite easy. However, before you decide whether to host with YouTube or Vimeo, you have a few things to consider.

YouTube has a much larger user base and is generally considered to be more mainstream and associated with social networking than Vimeo. Also, given that YouTube is owned by Google, it is heavily integrated with Google's suite of other products and its advertising platform. If you don't already have a Google account, you will need to set one up when registering for YouTube.

YouTube appears to have stricter guidelines on what audio can be used on your videos. This includes an automated system that scans your audio track for any music that may be protected by copyright. In some cases, you may be prevented from showing infringing videos on some or all types of devices. This can also include your video being unavailable in specific countries with stricter copyright laws. If you plan to use music in your *Minecraft* video, you should consider using royalty-free or self-published music to solve this issue.

TIP

Scratching the Itch to Twitch

Twitch has become a powerful force for sharing realtime gameplay—some broadcasters have hundreds of thousands of followers who tune in to watch their cool moves and amazing knowledge. With a free Turbo account, any videos you recard can be online for 60 days. It's an interesting idea that seems to have really taken off, but it's definitely not the same as creating a polished, carefully crafted video that can exist forever on YouTube or Vimeo. If you are interested, visit www.twitch.tv to learn more.

YouTube is well known for distracting advertisements that appear when viewed. There is a default 15-minute limit on the length of any video published; however, this can be extended at your request. This time limit is in place as another measure to combat copyright infringement.

Alternatively, Vimeo caters toward the more professional content producers and offers a cleaner and less cluttered interface. Different memberships are available, including a free account with some restrictions on video length, file size, and number of uploads.

Uploading Your Video

Depending on your choice of editing software, you may be given the option to publish your video directly to YouTube or Vimeo (you will need to log in to grant it permission). In the case where your editing software doesn't have this option, let's discuss how to upload your video manually.

First, if you don't already have a user account with Vimeo or YouTube, you will need to set one up. Thankfully, both platforms have made this process quite straightforward. As previously mentioned, if you already have a Google account or Gmail address, you are able to use this same account with YouTube, thus streamlining the process!

Once you are registered for your preferred platform, visit the appropriate site (www.vimeo.com) or (www.youtube.com) and then click **Login**. You will be taken to your home screen, which has an **Upload** button. From there, you are redirected to a page prompting you to choose your video file.

Depending on your browser and operating system versions, you should be able to select and upload multiple files at the same time. Alternatively, you can add individual files to a list for uploading.

Depending on the file size and speed of your Internet connection, the file(s) will proceed to upload (see Figure 10.10). Meanwhile, the user interface has been cleverly designed to allow you to edit and save details about your video while it is being uploaded in the background.

FIGURE 10.10 Uploading to Vimeo and YouTube is very similar. The interface varies slightly, but most of the information is the same.

Next, I'll go through some of the settings and info that can be edited for your video.

Basic Info

As the name implies, the Basic Info tab covers details such as the following:

- **Title**—This gets displayed as your main title in listings and at the top of the video, so make sure you keep it succinct but descriptive enough that people recognize its subject at a glance.

- **Description**—You can go into more detail here, with more information about the video and its contents.

- **Tags**—These are keywords that people might use to search for your video. "Minecraft" would be an important one to include, as well as any other specific words that relate to the content of your video. Try to put yourself in the position of the "searcher" and ask what words they might use to find you when looking at videos.

- **Credits**—If you have included music, or if you'd like to credit someone for helping you produce the video, you can do so here.

- **Thumbnail**—This is a very useful one. Once your video is uploaded, you can set what thumbnail or "still" is used when the video is not playing. This is also displayed in the general search results. It's important to use something that it is eye catching. Much like the description, it should give a good sense of the video at a glance. Vimeo will automatically choose a few thumbnails for you, but you also have the option to upload a completely independent image. Alternatively, the software allows you to "shuttle" to a specific frame in the video, and use that frame as the thumbnail. Pretty cool, right?

You will need to add a couple more settings and bits of information specific to Vimeo:

- **Privacy**—This is an important tab. You may prefer to share the video to a specific group of people or make it publically accessible. You can control the level of privacy attached to any individual video and also specify whether you allow it to be embedded into a web page or blog by other users.

- **Embed**—This tab will help you to control the appearance of your video player if you do decide to embed your videos into a web page or blog. You can preview how the player will look. Once you're happy with that, simply select **Get embed code** to generate a block of HTML code to drop into your website to display your videos *in situ*.

Adjust the settings to your liking. Once the upload is complete, the backend servers will do some post-processing of the video to make sure it's in the right format for all devices accessing it. This does take longer if you are using a free account, so if you're in a bit of a rush it's definitely worth upgrading your membership to ensure your videos are available considerably faster.

If you don't have time to wait around for the video to process once it has uploaded, you can actually close the browser and you'll receive an email when it is ready to view. Typically, you will also receive a direct link to the video to promote far and wide, encouraging people to come and watch your Minecrafting videos.

TIP

Why Should You Do All the Work?

If you are planning to upload a lot of videos, consider the Vimeo platform because it offers users the ability to import videos directly from your Dropbox folder. You'll need a Dropbox account; however, once you link Dropbox to Vimeo, any video files you drop into a designated folder on your PC will be picked up by Vimeo, processed automatically, and you'll receive an email notifying you as soon as the video is ready.

The Bottom Line

Not only are your *Minecraft* skills verging on extraordinary, you now have the tools to share your knowledge and adventures with the world. Record a video illustrating your wealth of survival tricks to help initiate newbies into the *Minecraft* fold and take other players on a flight of inspiration around your latest build.

In this chapter, we discussed some of your options for software and hardware video recording, as well as plotting camera paths using keyframes and flying, rolling, and focusing animation within your video. Adding titles and music will transform your edited video into an enviable piece of work that thousands of fellow Minecrafters can enjoy.

You have the tools, you have the knowledge—it's time to hit the lights!

Building Your Own Adventure

In This Chapter

- Explore Adventure mode.
- Do your initial planning and implementation.
- Master the command blocks.
- Use world-editing tools and helpers.
- Publish your own adventure.

Adventure mode provides a way to create a game within the game. From exemplary exploits to terrifying tribulations, you can create a world with its own rules and its own requirements to survive. Unleash a horde of zombies, fill the soundscape with deathly screams, or just provide a beautifully explorative experience based on peace and prosperity.

It's all within your control, and command blocks lead the way.

We're not going to build a complete world in this chapter, but I will give you the keys to unleash your imagination.

We'll start with an explanation of how Adventure mode differs from the standard *Minecraft* gameplay, then look at the incredible world editors that let you summon a landscape with terraforming powers.

Adventure mode protects the destruction of blocks, so dropping a player in a maze will leave them with no out but to find the path. It's all par for the course, of course, and this course can be whatever you make of it. Read on to learn how to construct, control, and produce an adventure of any kind (see Figure 11.1) that will leave players asking for more.

FIGURE 11.1 Get ready to embark on the ultimate adventure!

Adventure Mode

Adventure mode is typically turned on for downloadable adventure maps, or turned on by default on certain servers.

Playing such a map may require a new kind of ingenuity, especially to get through the first hour or so. You may have all the mob-swarming, explosive hazards of survival, but no ability to chop wood for a shelter unless you can find an axe that has been specifically configured to allow this. You can interact with blocks and objects (press buttons, use levers, and open doors and chests), but you may not be able to place blocks. Depending on the world's design, you might find yourself in an immediate fight for survival, running as fast as your little pixelated legs can carry you to find a village or similar structure for protection.

If you're a novice adventurer, enable cheats and/or bonus chests before creating a world to give yourself a head start. In Creative mode, use the command /**gamemode 2** to switch over to Adventure mode. Your best bet for on-the-fly supplies are found in villages and through trades, bonus chests, dungeons, spawn rooms, and treasure hoards.

TIP

A Gooey Zombie Center

An invisible wall maze with a surprise centerpiece is a delightfully nasty challenge for your players to navigate. Build the maze from barrier blocks gained using the command /**give <player> minecraft:barrier <amount>** in Creative mode (available from version 1.8). You'll see the blocks show up with a red outline, but they'll be invisible to your players in Adventure mode. Once your players finally reach the center of your maze to claim their reward, enlist a hidden dispenser of zombie spawners to chase them back out!

Initial Planning and Implementation

The inability to cheat has a higher purpose; Adventure mode is a brilliant map-sharing resource because it's much harder for players to destroy your hard-built creations. Before you decide what type of multiplayer map you're going to make, let's take a quick inventory of the most popular types:

- **Adventure maps**—Lead your players on a merry chase using instructional signs as they travel through your story-scape. The player becomes your main character and their mission unravels as they progress.

- **Game maps**—For the engineers and lateral thinkers, it's time to get serious about redstone. Build interactive games and complex challenges within your world such as defensive contraptions to fight attacking mobs, rail-coasters, mini-golf, and the art of the quick draw.

- **Survival maps**—This is the ultimate survival test, with minimal resources and plenty of challenges. You can really test your players' mettle with this one. Set your players' goals, leave chests full of booty in dark corners to find, or unleash the mob hordes you've been hiding in your basement on them!

- **Complete the monument maps**—A treasure hunt–styled map, where you hide collectibles within epic challenges with the players' aim of collecting them one by one to complete a central monument.

- **Creative maps**—If you've spent hours constructing a city to be envied, then why not show it off. Turn your creations into a *Minecraft* utopia for others to explore.

- **Player versus player**—Set the stage for players to battle it out in a hostile environment of your choosing. Plant zombie hordes to unite them in battle as well as treasure hordes to turn allies to foes. Last player standing wins.

- **Parkour maps**—Ready, set, go! Players race against each other to hit the finish line first, proving their perseverance and acrobatic skills as they jump through obstacles.

- **Puzzle maps**—Set up your players with a carnival of brainteasers by incorporating puzzles, traps, and mazes into your adventure world story. Keep it interesting by setting different levels of difficulty and rewarding the determination of your most clever players when they succeed.

So, What's Your Story?

Before you get stuck into building your own adventure, grab a pencil and create your story on paper. Seriously, doing this now will save you a *lot* of time compared to creating it on the fly. Include all of your ideas for clues, riddles, directional notes, rewards, goals and levels, and, most importantly, a backstory that your players can sink their teeth into. Why are they marooned on a desert island? How many clues will it take to solve the mystery? Who needs to be saved? Who awaits them in the tallest tower? What is their ultimate reward?

Think of each adventure challenge in turn and decide the best way to present it. Then draw everything out. Use grid paper if you're planning a complicated layout. Redstone mechanics may take time to build and require concealment. Again, although you may want to jump straight into building, this step will save you plenty of ground time.

Define your parameters early in the map-making process. You're the storyteller here, so you have to set ground rules for your players. If you're feeling particularly generous, you can actually give your players permission to destroy or use certain blocks for building. Think of the scenarios your players will find themselves in and consider how they'll behave. Here are some examples:

- If they come across a pickaxe, are they allowed to use it?
- Which type of blocks (if any) can they break?
- Do two or more players need to cooperate to pass a challenge?
- Do mobs drop items?
- Can players trade with villagers? If so, which items will they be offered?

TIP

Check for Updates

Make sure your map challenges are there to stay. Check for any software updates that might affect the way your map works and either incorporate them into your map in anticipation or find a workaround to suit your requirements.

Mastering Command Blocks

Adventure maps are part physical design (at least, virtually), and part automation through in-game scripting components. The scripting is achieved with command blocks that, when activated with redstone power, can perform a wide variety of actions. To give you an idea of some of the extraordinary capabilities of these, command blocks can do the following:

- Teleport players to a specific location
- Print messages in the chat window
- Change the time, difficulty, and weather
- Add or remove items from a player's inventory
- Create customized villagers that can sell any item in the game

- Create mob spawners
- Set potion effects upon players

First things, first: How do you get a command block? You must be in Creative mode, playing as operator on the server or as a single player with cheats enabled. The item ID for a command block is 137, so type in the following command:

```
/give <username> 137
```

When you place your command block and right-click it, you'll open the console command, which will be empty. This is where the magic happens. Essentially, you'll put in a string of commands to give yourself (or another player) an item (or items) or a set of rules attached to an item. Click **Done** to close your command window, and it's ready to use. In order to execute the command, you'll need to place a block directly next to it with a button or lever attached, or you can use a pressure plate on top or connect to a block via a redstone path.

Here, we are going to look at the way commands work, and we'll go through the most common basic commands. For a more comprehensive list of potential commands for your map, visit http://minecraft.gamepedia.com/Commands.

Breaking Down the Command String

You'll need to provide three parts to your command strings: selectors, commands, and specifiers. These parts are identified in Figure 11.2. We'll look at each component separately.

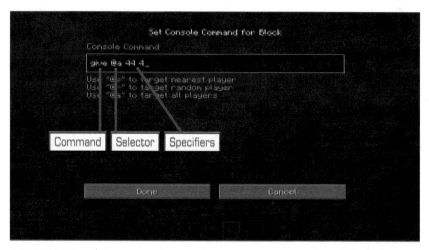

FIGURE 11.2 Each command has three basic components: the selector, the command, and the specifiers. Each component carries different information. As you become adept at setting commands, you can include multiple specifiers to narrow your results.

Selectors

The first thing to decide is who your command is for. Who gets the loot or punishment? You have three choices to include in your command; alternatively, you can simply type a specific player's name:

- **@p**—Used to target the nearest player to the command block

- **@r**—Used to target a random player on the server

- **@a**—Used to target all players on the server

Commands

Commands are just that: instructions for the world to act in a particular way on your player. You can give, clear, add, or take away XP (experience points) or levels, teleport, kill players (indirectly), and change the properties of items and potions, among other things.

In the list of sample commands that follows, take note that the items in angled-brackets (< and >) require a value input to make the command work, whereas the square brackets indicate that the enclosed information is optional—that is, your command will still work without this information. Here are a couple examples:

- **[Amount]**—How many of this particular item/action do you want? Include it as a number with spaces on either side. If you don't specify otherwise, the default amount will be for one single item or action. You can only give the maximum of that item that fits in a stack, but using the value -1 will create an item that's infinite.

- **[Data]**—For many items in your inventory, there are multiples of the same type, different only by their color, texture, and so on. These items (for example, different colors for glass panes, clay, wool, or variations of sandstone, flowers, and so on) each have a "data" number after their item ID that is used to identify them. In this case, enter the item ID number, followed by a space, then the data number. For example, for a brick slab, you would enter **44 4**.

Items are specified using their ID number or name. Find the full list at http://minecraft.gamepedia.com/Data_values/Item_IDs (http://goo.gl/J0af4G).

Listed here are some of the most helpful commands for creating an adventure:

- Give items to your players, either as a reward or challenge:

  ```
  give <player> <item> [amount] [data]
  ```

- Remove items from your players:

  ```
  clear [player] [item] [data]
  ```

  (Unless you specify which item you want to clear as a [data] value, the entire inventory will be removed. For a specific [data] item, the total amount will always be cleared.)

- Create an instant mob infestation or clear the decks:

  ```
  difficulty <new difficulty>
  ```

  (Here, 0 equals peaceful, 1 is easy, 2 is normal, and 3 is hard. You can use this command to instantly remove the hostile mobs in-game at the press of a button.)

- Use the game mode command to switch your players between modes as part of your adventure story:

  ```
  gamemode <mode> [player]
  ```

  (Here, 0 is Survival mode, 1 is Creative mode, and 2 is Adventure mode.)

- Keep your players engaged throughout their journey. Use the say command to leave messages for your players as they progress through the map:

  ```
  say <player> <message>
  ```

  You can use your selector to specify who the message is for by incorporating their name in the message.

- Send a private message.

  ```
  tell <player> <message>
  ```

  This command is the same as say, but your message will be sent as a private "whisper" to the player intended. Use your own name and place the command block near your front door and use your own name to create a type of alarm system.

- There and back again:

  ```
  spawnpoint
  spawnpoint <player> <x y z co-ordinates>
  ```

  Use the first command to set the command block's position as the new spawn point, or include specific x/y/z coordinates to set it elsewhere.

- Keep your players on their toes by setting triggers that switch between day and night.

  ```
  time set <value>
  ```

  Each in-game hour is 1,000 hours, so your 24-hour day is made up of 24,000 MC units. Day equals 1,000, and night is 13,000.

- Jump through your day with the flick of a switch:

  ```
  time add <value>
  ```

- Teleport your players from one challenge to the next. Keep in mind that you'll need to find out the specific coordinates first if there's a particular landmark/trap/chest you want them to appear at, and to not teleport them into the ground or too high in the air, although could be fun too.

  ```
  tp <player> <x y z co-ordinates>
  ```

- Variations to a standard teleport include the following:

  - `tp @p @r @r` will teleport one or two random players to the other.

  - `tp @a @p` will teleport all players to the player closest to the command block.

  - `tp @a[l=<value>]`, where `l` equals any player with a maximum of `<value>` experience levels.

  - `tp @a[lm=<value>]`, where `lm` is the minimum level of experience for each player.

- To narrow your results, you can target your players within a certain experience range by combining both values in a command such as the following:

  `tp @a[l=<value>,lm=<value>]`

- Rain, hail, or shine. Set your trigger to clear, rain, or thunder to change the atmosphere of the gameplay to suit each challenge:

  `weather <value> [duration in seconds]`

- Level the playing field. This command allows you to give or remove experience points or levels to or from players. If you're removing levels from your players, add a negative sign in front of the amount.

  `xp <amount> [player]`
  `xp <amount>L [player]`

- It's your story! There are a number of different game rules you can include as commands, and each requires a value input of either `true` or `false` to work:

  `gamerule <rulename> [value]`

  Game rule commands can include the following:

  - **`commandBlockOutput`**—This command will enable or disable the display text on a command block in a multiplayer environment. Set this to `false` so your players don't get the command screen each time it's triggered.

  - **`doFireTick`**—Use this command to specify whether a fire is going to spread and extinguish naturally (as opposed to stay burning in one spot when set to `false`).

  - **`doMobLoot`**—If this command is set to `true`, mobs drop their loot when killed for collection by the player. If it's set to `false`, no such luck!

  - **`doMobSpawning`**—If this command is set to `true`, mobs will naturally spawn in your world. If it's set to `false`, your players can get a good night's sleep (that is, unless you spawn creeper eggs beside their bed).

- **doTileDrops**—If this command is set to `false`, blocks won't drop if they are mined in Survival mode, so no reward for your players' inventory. (Although players don't have a default ability to mine in Adventure mode, you can create an exception rule on this.)

- **keepInventory**—Be like a Nazgul and wield your sword after death. This is a good rule to set to `true` for beginners to help them out. The immortal stash will include players' inventory items, armor, and experience points.

- **mobGriefing**—If this command is set to `false`, your world won't suffer damage if your mobs blow up; they can't pick up or change blocks in any way.

Specifiers

Including a specifier in your command puts added limitations on the result. You can specify parameters such as the distance of a player from the command block, and you can filter out players based on XP level, type, player team, game mode, and so on.

You can add a specifier to any command that contains `@`. Include your specifiers in square brackets at the end of your command. Here are a few examples of how a specifier might work.

Teleporting to a Central Point

Perhaps you'd like to teleport your players to a central point:

- Radius:

  `tp @a[r=<value>]`

  Here, `r` is the number of blocks (radius) from the command block (in other words, all players within a specific area).

- Minimum radius:

  `tp @p[rm=<value>]`

  Here, `rm` is the minimum distance from the command block (in other words, all players outside of a specified area).

If you want get a bit fancy, you can include external coordinates (away from the command block). For example, you can use `tp @a[x,y,z,r]` to summon all players within a radius (`r`) of `<value>` blocks from place `x,y,z` on your map (see Figure 11.3 and Figure 11.4).

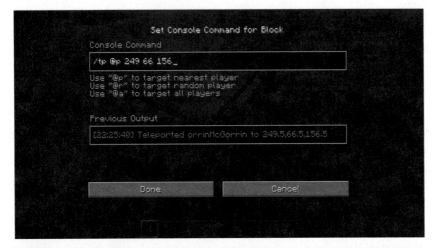

FIGURE 11.3 Use the `teleport` command to move players through your game by specifying coordinates to send them to.

FIGURE 11.4 Out of the frying pan.... Set up booby traps and challenges for your players to face on the other end of their teleport, like this zombie spawn dungeon.

Using `effect` Commands

Need to up the stakes? Although you can't use a kill command within a command block, you can kill your players indirectly using an `effect` command, as shown in Figure 11.5:

```
effect <player> <effect> [amplifier] [seconds]
```

Here, the effect ID denotes which affect your player receives and then how many seconds it lasts.

FIGURE 11.5 Use the Instant Damage effect (ID 7) at 10× normal strength for 15 seconds for an easy kill. Here's an example:

```
effect @p 7 10 15
```

When this effect command is triggered, the player must start again (see Figure 11.6).

FIGURE 11.6 Hide this simple kill command for an unsuspecting player to stumble across.

NOTE

You Can Add All the Specifiers You Like

You can keep adding specifiers to your command to restrict your search; just remember to separate each specifier with a comma (and close off your brackets!).

Rewarding Players

Feeling generous? Let's look at a specifier that can be used to reward your players. Let's isolate all players in, say, Adventure mode, and reward them with a second-breakfast of five apples (item 260 in our inventory):

```
give @a[m=<gamemode>] <item> [amount] where m=gamemode
(0=survival,1=creative,2=adventure)
```

Therefore, our example would become give@a[m=2] 260 5.

TIP

Make Sure to Set Your Trap Correctly

Remember, pressure plates, slabs, and other "part" blocks still take up a whole block of virtual space. If you use a command block to spawn a player on a pressure plate to trip a booby trap, make sure you set the coordinates to one block above the plate. They'll fall onto it as they spawn, setting off the trigger.

The Comparator

Instead of creating an output message such as the /say and /tell commands, your command block can also output to a comparator. Whenever a command block executes a command, the comparator connected to it will output the result by igniting a redstone trail across the blocks adjacent to it to match its signal strength.

This redstone trail will indicate how your game is progressing. For example, you could see how many players were affected by your command or are currently in a specified area (see Figure 11.7). You could also use a command to get an indication of how many players have a high XP level or are carrying certain items in their inventory.

If you don't want to impact your players directly, you can determine this output through your command block using the /testfor specifier. For example, let's test for all of the players in gamemode (m) Creative (1) that are between a 10-to-20-block radius from coordinates x,y,z:

```
testfor @a[x,y,z,rm=10,r=20,m=1]
```

Your comparator will output a Redstone trail equivalent in length to the number of players that fall into your targeted group.

FIGURE 11.7   There are two redstone ignitions in the trail, which implies that there are two players within the 10–20 block radius used in the sample command.

testfor is a really useful command to keep an eye on the game progress of a multiplayer map.

The tellraw Command

You can use the tellraw code command with the chat function instead of using the say and tell commands. Using tellraw offers more advanced ways of communicating with your players. You can input this command directly into your command block, the same as those shown earlier.

The more elements you want to include in your command, the longer your command will be. There is a standard template for adding new elements to a command, a bit like adding descriptive words in a sentence to make it more meaningful. It takes a bit of practice, but it's well worth the effort!

For example, you may want to set a command block to have a message appear when your player triggers it. Let's get a little fancier. We'll work through this example by showing each new element added in bold text so you can see how the command sentence is constructed.

Here's our basic message shown in the command block in Figure 11.8, followed by the resulting chat screen in Figure 11.9:

```
tellraw @a {"text":"Congratulations! You survived the zombie
apocalypse!"}
```

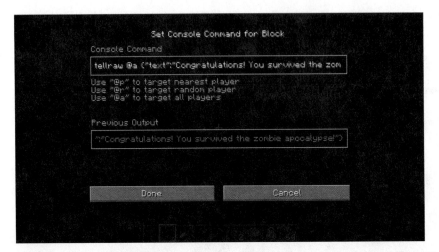

FIGURE 11.8 Right-click your command block and then enter the `tellraw` command in the top pane.

FIGURE 11.9 The message appears in the chat screen of the intended player.

Now let's change the color of our text by adding another element to the command:

```
tellraw @a {"text":"Congratulations! You survived the zombie
apocalypse!","color":"red"}
```

We can see the resulting message appear in Figure 11.10, with red text.

FIGURE 11.10 Change the color of the text by adding a `color` element into your command string.

If you'd like to add more text to your message, repeat the preceding string with your new text (and optional new color) within the brackets and separate them by adding "extra" between the commands, as shown in Figure 11.11. Remember, every time you add a bracket, you must close it again before the end of your command.

```
tellraw @a {"text":"Congratulations! You survived the zombie apocalypse!"
,"color":"red","extra":[{ "text":"Your reward is hidden somewhere in the
castle!","color":"gold"}]}
```

FIGURE 11.11 You can include multiple instructions by adding extra text elements.

Now let's make the extra text hover instead. First, we add a `hoverEvent` to the existing string (as always, separated by a comma):

```
tellraw @a {"text": "Congratulations! You survived the zombie
apocalypse!","color": "red","hoverEvent": {"action": "show_text","value":
"Your reward is hidden somewhere in the castle!"}}
```

In the chat pane, we can see the extra message if we hover over the text, as shown in Figure 11.12.

FIGURE 11.12   The hover feature is great for hiding "bonus" text.

Now, let's add an action to send our player on the next challenge of our map. We'll teleport the player inside our medieval castle for a treasure hunt (see Figure 11.13). Keep in mind that to command a teleport, you'll need to know the landing coordinates first.

```
tellraw @a {"text": "Congratulations! You survived the zombie
apocalypse!","color": "red","hoverEvent": {"action": "show_text","value": "Your
reward is hidden somewhere in the castle!"},"clickEvent": {"action": "run_
command","value": "/tp @p x y z"}}
```

There are plenty of fun additions you can include using the `tellraw` command. For more elements, visit the complete list at http://minecraft.gamepedia.com/Commands. If you're having trouble getting it to work right, try using a tellraw generator like the one created by Ezekiel, which can be found at http://ezekielelin.com/tellraw/.

FIGURE 11.13 The teleport feature is a fun way to switch the players between challenges on your map.

World-Editing Tools and Helpers (Map the Middle Kingdom)

Gameplay (puzzles and obstacles), storyline, and scenery are all important aspects of a good map. The aim is to make your adventure map challenging for players, but still user friendly and fun to explore.

You saw in Chapter 5, "Advanced Construction," that programs such as MCEdit, World Painter, World Edit, and Voxel Sniper will allow you to alter the physical attributes of your adventure map by adding 3D shapes and custom imports, terraforming (making a mountain, digging an ocean), and painting (changing snow to forest, and back again). You can change the size of individual landmarks, flatten, remove, or expand sections, and create custom monster and mob skins.

If you have some epic ideas for modding your adventure map, but don't have the programming experience to get there, try using a tool such as http://mcreator.pylo.si/ to help you build them. You can create new blocks, dimensions, recipes, foods, mobs, plants, biomes, and many other elements to bring your adventure story to life.

Also, plenty of standard mods are available that can help customize your map. If you do use additional mods or texture packs in your adventure map that are helpful to the player, make sure you include a link in your description so that players can download the mods and still use the map successfully.

Here are some examples of mod features you can use to bolster your mapping tool belt:

- Edit your players to have custom-shaped body parts.
- Craft heavy-duty explosives, missiles, flares, and bombs.
- Change the name and author on decorative books.
- Add enchantments to any item.
- Craft orbs to super-grow plants or set fire to things, explode, set off lightning striked, and freeze and dry blocks.
- Set wool blocks to fall when unsupported, like sand or gravel.
- Create custom shops for your villages.
- Bulk-fill dispensers with any item.
- Customize your potion's color, strength, and effects.
- Apply enchantments to standard inventory items.
- Craft orbs to convert Overworld blocks to nether blocks.
- Change to "Sandbox" mode so you can test changes to your world without saving them (for example, major destructions).
- Reduce fall damage and spawn mobs using orbs.
- Customize the detection capabilities of spawners.
- Edit the names of items in your inventory.
- Alter your mob's destructive power, speed, and spawning locations.
- And many, many more....

Publishing Your Own Adventure (Terrifying Noobs)

The best part of creating an adventure map is, of course, sharing it. There is a massive community of mapmakers and enthusiasts who will jump at your challenges, so don't be shy in joining.

Before you upload your map, test it thoroughly. Make sure all your signposts, triggers, redstone, commands, and challenges work the way they're meant to.

To share your map, first you'll need to compress the file into either a .rar or .zip file so that it's a fast download for your players. Find the map by searching the saves folder in your computer's .minecraft folder.

Upload your map to a file-sharing service such as Mediafire or Dropbox; then include the link in the upload form on one of the map-sharing community sites. Make sure you follow the specific rules set by each site.

Here are some of the fantastic online communities where you can share your adventures:

- www.minecraftmaps.com
- www.planetminecraft.com
- www.minecraftforum.net
- www.minecraftworldshare.com

Take a few screen captures of your completed map and post them on your map profile. Add a summary of the best features and challenges so that your players have an idea of what to expect. Make sure you include any positive reviews you receive, and take the opportunity to use negative (constructive) feedback to improve your adventure.

NOTE

Griefing

Although the majority of mods are harmless, some are created specifically to do damage in multiplayer worlds. So-called "griefers" sometimes form teams to execute the most damage they can using modified items, such as exploding masses of TNT in buildings, setting uncontrollable fires, or creating server lags by excess mob spawning, redstone drops, and chat spamming, among other things. You can protect your server by installing an anti-griefer plug-in by Bukkit (www.bukkit.org). If necessary, use a rollback/login plug-in to undo damage done by griefers during multiplayer gaming. It's a good idea to limit the more destructive resources in your adventure map (such as lava, TNT, spawners, and fire spread) so that unfamiliar players behave themselves.

The Bottom Line

Creating an adventure map is a fantastic way of extending your favorite challenges to a multiplayer environment. Build, create, conquer! Use the opportunity to hone your redstone and puzzle-building skills, showcase your magnificent constructions, and provide a unique experience for other players.

Use world-editing tools to terraform your map into a story-scape worthy of legend. You can re-create the twisting tunnels of Moria and set a mob-ambush on your players as they battle for precious items, or you can take your adventures to the sky within an epic arena of brain-crunching puzzles, mazes, and death-defying jumps.

The possibilities are limitless, so choose your own adventure and begin an unexpected journey!

INDEX

Symbols

A

B

G

S

REGISTER THIS PRODUCT
SAVE 35%*
ON YOUR NEXT PURCHASE!

How to Register Your Product

- Go to quepublishing.com/register
- Sign in or create an account
- Enter the 10- or 13-digit ISBN that appears on the back cover of your product

Benefits of Registering

- Ability to download product updates
- Access to bonus chapters and workshop files
- A 35% coupon to be used on your next purchase – valid for 30 days
    - To obtain your coupon, click on "Manage Codes" in the right column of your Account page
- Receive special offers on new editions and related Que products

Please note that the benefits for registering may vary by product. Benefits will be listed on your Account page under Registered Products.

We value and respect your privacy. Your email address will not be sold to any third party company.

* 35% discount code presented after product registration is valid on most print books, eBooks, and full-course videos sold on QuePublishing.com. Discount may not be combined with any other offer and is not redeemable for cash. Discount code expires after 30 days from the time of product registration. Offer subject to change.

quepublishing.com

Other Books
YOU MIGHT LIKE!

ISBN: 9780789753601

ISBN: 9780789751850

ISBN: 9780789751959

SAVE 30%
Use discount code **MINECRAFT**

Visit **quepublishing.com** to learn more!

* Discount code MINECRAFT is valid for a 30% discount off the list price of eligible titles purchased on informit.com or quepublishing.com. Coupon not valid on book + eBook bundles. Discount code may not be combined with any other offer and is not redeemable for cash. Offer subject to change.

ALWAYS LEARNING

PEARSON

MAKE THE MOST OF YOUR SMARTPHONE, TABLET, COMPUTER, AND MORE!

My iPad
SIXTH EDITION

COVERS
iOS 7 for iPad Air, 3rd/4th generation, iPad 2, and iPad mini

Gary Rosenzweig

que

ISBN 13: 9780789751027

My iMovie

Craig James Johnston
Cheryl Brumbaugh-Duncan

que

ISBN 13: 9780789749956

My Samsung Galaxy S5

Steve Schwartz
with Craig James Johnston

que

ISBN 13: 9780789753496

My Xbox One

Bill Loguidice
Christina T. Loguidice

que

ISBN 13: 9780789751959

Full-Color, Step-by-Step Guides

The "My..." series is a visually rich, task-based series to help you get up and running with your new device and technology and tap into some of the hidden, or less obvious features. The organized, task-based format allows you to quickly and easily find exactly the task you want to accomplish, and then shows you how to achieve it with minimal text and plenty of visual cues.

Visit quepublishing.com/mybooks to learn more about the My... book series from Que.

que

quepublishing.com